Karin Linhart

Englische Rechtssprache – Ein Studien- und Arbeitsbuch

Englische Rechtssprache
Ein Studien- und Arbeitsbuch

von
Karin Linhart

unter Mitarbeit von
Corin Stone
U.S. Government, Washington, D.C./USA

Verlag C. H. Beck oHG, München
Manz'sche Verlags- und Universitätsbuchhandlung, Wien
Helbing Lichtenhahn, Basel
2008

Über die Autorin
Dr. Karin Linhart, LL.M. (Duke) ist Akademische Rätin an der Juristischen
Fakultät der Julius-Maximilians-Universität Würzburg. Sie unterrichtet neben
dem deutschen Zivilrecht Veranstaltungen zur englischen Rechtssprache, zum
US-amerikanischen Recht in englischer Sprache und zum Recht im südlichen
Afrika. Darüber hinaus leitet sie das Fachsprachenprogramm der Juristischen
Fakultät der Universität Würzburg.

Website: http://www.jura.uni-wuerzburg.de/lehrstuehle/professoren/
linhart/dr_linhart/

C. H. Beck ISBN 978-3-406-56878-7
Manz ISBN 978-3-214-00512-2
Helbing Lichtenhahn ISBN 978-3-7190-2743-8

© 2008 Verlag C.H. Beck oHG, München
Wilhelmstr. 9, 80801 München
Druck und Bindung: Nomos Verlagsgesellschaft
In den Lissen 12, 76547 Sinzheim
Satz: ottomedien, Darmstadt
Gedruckt auf säurefreiem, alterungsbeständigem Papier
(hergestellt aus chlorfrei gebleichtem Zellstoff)

Für D.

Vorwort

Dieses Studien- und Arbeitsbuch ist für einen weiten Kreis von Interessenten an der englischen Fachsprache geeignet: Es ist zum einen gedacht für Studenten der Rechtswissenschaften, die sich auf die Klausur oder die mündliche Prüfung zum Erwerb eines fachspezifischen Fremdsprachennachweises oder auf ein Auslandspraktikum oder Auslandsstudium vorbereiten. Zum anderen richtet es sich auch an Studierende der Wirtschafts- und Politikwissenschaften, die als Neben- oder Wahlpflichtfach Rechtswissenschaften gewählt haben und in diesem Zusammenhang auch Kenntnisse in der englischen rechtswissenschaftlichen Terminologie erwerben möchten. Darüber hinaus eignet es sich für Rechtsreferendare bei der Vorbereitung der Wahlstation im Ausland sowie für alle Praktiker zur Auffrischung oder zum Aufbau ihrer Kenntnisse der englischen Fachterminologie, die im Zuge der Europäisierung und Internationalisierung rechtlicher Sachverhalte heute für das berufliche Weiterkommen von großer Bedeutung sind.

Die meisten der hier eingebrachten Materialien sind bereits seit mehreren Semestern erfolgreich praktisch erprobt. Sie dienten als Vorlesungsmaterial der Veranstaltungen Rechtsenglisch I und Rechtsenglisch II an der Juristischen Fakultät der Universität Würzburg. Wiederholungen sind bewusst eingebaut, um neben der Motivation letztlich den Lernerfolg zu optimieren.

Sicherheit im Umgang mit der englischen Fachterminologie ist heute unablässig. Dennoch kommen diese Kenntnisse und der sichere Umgang mit englischen juristischen Texten nicht automatisch. Mit dem Erwerb dieses Buches haben Sie den ersten Schritt getan. Ich möchte Sie ermutigen, sich Zeit zu nehmen und sich in die einzelnen Kapitel zu vertiefen. Nehmen Sie sich Einheit für Einheit vor, wiederholen Sie das Gelernte direkt im Anschluss und weitere Male auch noch nach längerer Zeit. Nutzen Sie auch weitere Möglichkeiten, sich der englischen Fachsprache zu widmen. Am Ende des Buches sind Angaben zu juristischen und nicht-juristischen Websites mit Informationen zu den USA, Kanada, Indien, Großbritannien, Südafrika, Nigeria oder Namibia im Internet enthalten. Binden Sie die englische Sprache am besten täglich in Ihren Tagesablauf ein, und Sie werden schon nach wenigen Wochen feststellen, dass es Ihnen immer leichter fällt und sogar Spaß bereitet, sich auf Englisch informieren zu können.

Der Gedanke zu diesem Buch und der Beginn der Erstellung der Materialien gehen bereits gute zwei Jahre zurück. Ich freue mich ganz besonders, jetzt den Menschen danken zu können, die zu seinem Gelingen beigetragen haben: Der erste große Dank gebührt meiner Lektorin beim Verlag C.H. Beck, Frau Hauptmann, deren profunde Sachkunde und natürliche Freundlichkeit mich begeistert haben. Es hat großen Spaß gemacht, mit Ihnen zusammenzuarbeiten. Vielen Dank!

Weitere Anerkennung und Dank möchte ich meinen hervorragenden studentischen Hilfskräften, stellvertretend Laura Alester, Patrick Leimig, Anja Schmidt und Petra Zangl, aussprechen, die im frühen Stadium ihres Studiums bereits große Sorgfalt bewiesen und hervorragende Arbeit vor allem beim Formatieren, Recherchieren und Korrekturlesen geleistet haben.

Weitere Menschen haben ganz zu Beginn und in der Endphase der Erstellung des Buches wertvolle Beiträge geleistet: Ich danke Beate Silva für die sprachliche

Durchsicht der ersten Texte. Maya Mandery danke ich nicht nur für die sorgfältige und zuverlässige Durchsicht des Manuskripts und die wertvollen Anmerkungen und Verbesserungsvorschläge, sondern auch für die großartige Unterstützung vor und hinter den Kulissen des Fachsprachenprogramms der Juristischen Fakultät der Universität Würzburg. Nicht nur für die Ermutigung und Motivation bei der Erstellung dieses Buches danke ich Katharina Ruf und Thorsten Hermsmeyer. Eure Unterstützung ist von unschätzbarem Wert. Ich danke Euch!

Danken möchte ich auch unserem Dekan, Herrn Professor Dr. Frank Zieschang, der mich in der Phase der Fertigstellung angespornt und mir den zeitlichen Rahmen eingeräumt hat, das Manuskript in recht kurzer Zeit fertigzustellen. Eine solche Unterstützung ist nicht selbstverständlich und ich weiß sie sehr zu schätzen.

In den letzten Tagen der Fertigstellung des Manuskripts standen mir auch Angelika Faul, Rebekka Josupeit, Caroline Rupp und Hannes Reiher mit Rat und Tat und größtem Einsatz zur Seite. Ganz herzlichen Dank dafür. Nicht zuletzt danke ich meinen Studenten an der Juristischen Fakultät der Universität Würzburg, die mir mit guten Fragen und Anmerkungen geholfen haben, die Materialien dieses Buches immer weiter zu entwickeln.

Würzburg, im August 2007   Karin Linhart

Inhaltsübersicht

Inhaltsverzeichnis

A. General Legal Terms

I. Common Law and Civil Law Traditions

a) Text

The law in England, Wales, and the United States differs widely from German law. The law of these countries is based on the common law legal tradition, whereas German Law is based on the civil law legal tradition. Other countries based on the common law system include Ireland, Canada (except Quebec), India, and New Zealand. Countries that follow the civil law system include France and Spain. Some countries, like South Africa for example, have a hybrid legal system. The term hybrid legal system refers to a system that incorporates elements of both the common law and civil law.

In common law countries, the primary source of law is case law. This means that law is developed on a case-by-case basis. A court decision that is binding to lower courts is called a precedent. The development of the law on a case-by-case basis provides common law countries with a high degree of flexibility and is capable of reflecting changes in society, new inventions and changing needs. In the common law system a distinction is drawn between law and equity – something that is rather unknown in the civil law tradition. English common law was adopted by most English colonies. Sir William Blackstone's Commentaries on the Laws of England, completed in 1769, had their share in anchoring English common law in the New World. Since then, however, US common law has developed independently from its English origin. Today, the US and England can be considered two distinct legal systems.

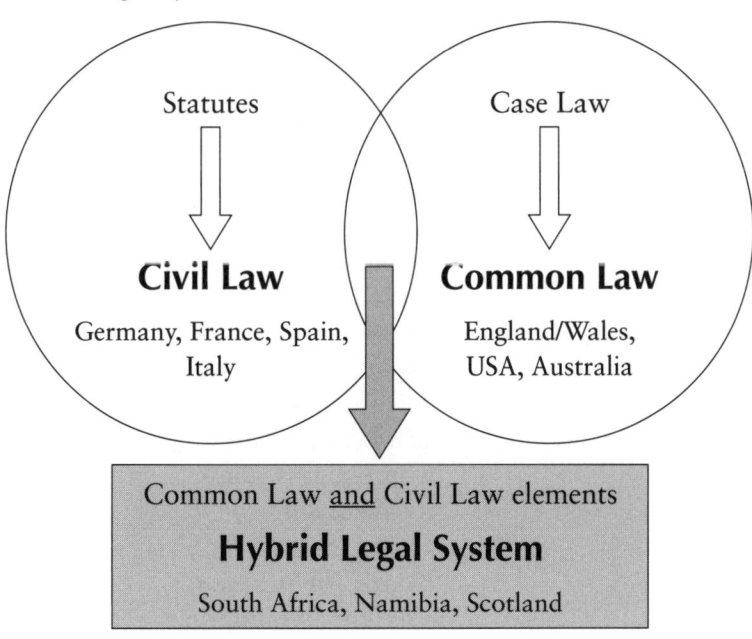

In civil law countries, the law is based predominantly on statutes. The civil law tradition is derived from Roman law. Civil law provides the framework for most legal systems in continental Europe and South and Central America. In the United States, only Louisiana has a legal system based on the civil law tradition. In the United Kingdom, Scottish law was influenced by Roman law and as a result, Scotland has a hybrid legal system.

b) Vokabeln zum Text

adopt, to	annehmen, übernehmen, rezipieren
anchor, to	verankern
as a result	infolgedessen, im Ergebnis
be based on, to	begründet sein auf, basieren
binding court decision	bindende gerichtliche Entscheidung
both ... and ...	sowohl ... als auch ...
case law	Fallrecht, Rechtsprechung
commentary	Kommentar
common law	*siehe unten*
complete, to	fertigstellen
consider, to	erachten, ansehen als, berücksichtigen
court	Gericht
court decision	Gerichtsentscheidung
degree	Grad
derive from, to	stammen von, sich ableiten von
differ, to	sich unterscheiden
distinct	unterschiedlich
draw a distinction, to	unterscheiden, differenzieren
Equity	*siehe unten*
except	außer
framework	Rahmen
however	jedoch
hybrid	hybrid, gemischt
include, to	beinhalten
incorporate, to	umfassen, verbinden
independent	unabhängig
influence, to	beeinflussen
judge made law	Richterrecht
law	Recht (*siehe unten*)
legal system	Rechtssystem
legal tradition	Rechtskreis
precedent	Präzedenzfall
predominantly	überwiegend
provide for, to	darstellen, bereitstellen
provide with, to	versorgen mit, bereitstellen
refer to, to	sich beziehen auf
Roman law	Römisches Recht
source of law	Rechtsquelle
statute	Gesetz
term	Begriff (*siehe unten*)
whereas	während, wohingegen

c) Erläuterung der Fachterminologie

Der Begriff *law* hat zwei Bedeutungen: Zum einen das „Recht" in seiner Gesamtheit und zum anderen „Gesetz" (dann Synonym für *statute*). Um welche Bedeutung es sich handelt, muss dem jeweiligen Zusammenhang entnommen werden.

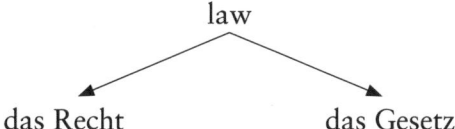

Der deutsche Begriff „**Gesetz**" hat im Englischen noch eine weitere, also insgesamt **drei Entsprechungen**. Dies ist neben *law* und *statute* der Begriff *act*. *Act* wird dann groß geschrieben, wenn auf ein bestimmtes Gesetz Bezug genommen wird (z. B. *Patriots Act*).

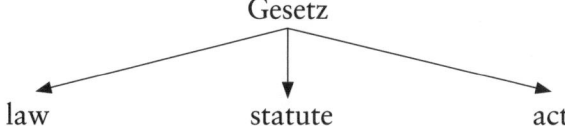

Die beiden Bezeichnungen für die Rechtskreise *common law* und *civil law* bleiben im Deutschen (wie in den meisten anderen Sprachen) unübersetzt.

Der Begriff *common law* hat **drei Bedeutungen**: Zum einen kann er sich auf einen der beiden großen Rechtskreise beziehen, also im Gegensatz zu *civil law* verwendet werden. Dann wiederum kann sich hinter *common law* ein Synonym für *case law* verstecken. Das *common law* grenzt sich dann als Fallrecht im Bereich der Rechtsquellen vom Gesetzesrecht (*statutory law*) ab. Ein weiterer Begriff für Recht, das von der Rechtsprechung entwickelt wird, ist *judge-made law*. Letztlich kann *common law* im Gegensatz zu *Equity* stehen. *Equity* entwickelte sich im 12. Jahrhundert als Gegenpol zum starren, unflexiblen (*common*) *law*. Im Rahmen der *Equity* wurden immer dann neue Rechtsbehelfe geschaffen, wenn die Möglichkeiten, die das (*common*) *law* den Parteien eines Rechtsstreits bot, als unbillig oder unfair erachtet wurden.

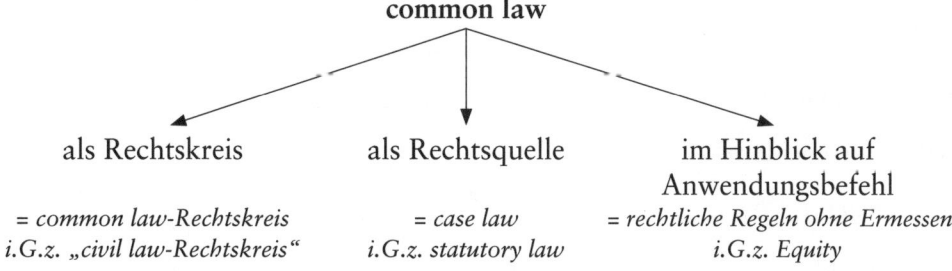

Der Begriff *Equity* kann klein oder groß geschrieben werden. Er entspricht im Großen und Ganzen dem deutschen Begriff „Billigkeitsrecht", hat aber im *common law*-Rechtskreis eine viel tiefgreifendere Bedeutung. Daher sollte der Begriff *Equity* am besten unübersetzt bleiben, um dessen eigenständige Bedeutung herauszustellen.

d) Lernkontrolle

Bitte ergänzen Sie die englischen Begriffe:

annehmen, übernehmen, rezipieren	_____
beeinflussen	_____
Begriff (2×)	a) *term* b) *notion*
begründet sein auf, basieren	_____
bindende gerichtliche Entscheidung	_____
erachten, ansehen als, berücksichtigen	_____
Fallrecht, Rechtsprechung	_____
Gericht	_____
Gerichtsentscheidung	_____
Gesetz (3×)	a) _____ b) _____
	c) _____
hybrides/gemischtes Rechtssystem	_____
infolgedessen, im Ergebnis	_____
jedoch	_____
Präzedenzfall	_____
Rahmen	_____
Recht	_____
Rechtskreis	_____
Rechtsquelle	_____
Rechtssystem	_____
Richterrecht	_____
sich beziehen auf	_____
sich unterscheiden	_____
überwiegend	_____
unabhängig	_____
unterscheiden, differenzieren	_____
während, wohingegen	_____

Lösung siehe S. 115

II. Areas of Law

a) Text und Übung

In most legal systems, the law is divided into public law and private law. These are further divided into distinct areas of law, such as constitutional law, commercial law, or family law. Due to differences in the structure in different legal systems, sometimes areas of law in one legal system have no equivalent in other legal systems.

Übung: Bitte ordnen Sie soweit möglich den englischen Begriffen die entsprechenden deutschen Bezeichnungen der Rechtsgebiete in dem grau unterlegten Kasten zu.

1. administrative law	Verwaltungsrecht	(Individual-)Arbeitsrecht
2. antitrust	_____	Deliktsrecht
3. civil procedure	_____	Erbrecht
4. commercial law	_____	Europ. Gemeinschaftsrecht
5. company law	_____	Familienrecht
6. comparative law	_____	Gesellschaftsrecht
7. conflict of laws	_____	Gewerblicher Rechtsschutz
8. constitutional law	_____	Internationales Privatrecht
9. contracts	_____	Kartellrecht
10. copyright law	_____	Kollektives Arbeitsrecht
11. criminal law	_____	Kriminologie
12. criminal procedure	_____	Patentrecht
13. criminology		Rechtsgeschichte
14. E.C. law	_____	Rechtsphilosophie
15. employment law	_____	Rechtsvergleichung
16. environmental law	_____	Sachenrecht
17. family law	_____	Schuldrecht
18. intellectual property	_____	Steuerrecht
19. labo(u)r law	_____	Strafprozessrecht
20. law of obligations	_____	Strafrecht
21. law of succession	_____	Umweltrecht

22. legal history	_____	Ungerechtfertigte Bereicherung
23. legal philosophy	_____	Unlauterer Wettbewerb
24. patent law	_____	Urheberrecht
25. property	_____	Verfassungsrecht
26. public international law	_____	Vertragsrecht
27. tax law	_____	~~Verwaltungsrecht~~
28. torts	_____	Völkerrecht
29. unfair competition	_____	Wirtschaftsrecht
30. unjust enrichment	_____	Zivilprozessrecht

Lösung siehe S. 116

b) Vokabeln zum Text

administrative law	Verwaltungsrecht
antitrust	Kartellrecht
area of law	Rechtsgebiet
be divided, to	unterteilt sein
civil procedure	Zivilprozessrecht
commercial law	Wirtschaftsrecht (*siehe unten*)
company law	Gesellschaftsrecht
comparative law	Rechtsvergleichung
conflict of laws	Internationales Privatrecht (*siehe unten*)
constitutional law	Verfassungsrecht
contracts	Vertragsrecht (*siehe unten*)
copyright law	Urheberrecht
criminal law	Strafrecht
criminal procedure	Strafprozessrecht
criminology	Kriminologie
due to	aufgrund, wegen
E.C. law	Europäisches Gemeinschaftsrecht
employment law	(Individual-)Arbeitsrecht
environmental law	Umweltrecht
equivalent	Entsprechung, Pendant
family law	Familienrecht
intellectual property	Gewerblicher Rechtsschutz
labo(u)r law	Kollektives Arbeitsrecht (*siehe unten*)
law of obligations	Schuldrecht (*siehe unten*)
law of succession	Erbrecht (*siehe unten*)
legal history	Rechtsgeschichte
legal philosophy	Rechtsphilosophie
legal system	Rechtssystem
patent law	Patentrecht
private law	Privatrecht

property	Sachenrecht (*siehe unten*)
public international law	Völkerrecht
public law	Öffentliches Recht
tax law	Steuerrecht
torts	Deliktsrecht (*siehe unten*)
unfair competition	Unlauterer Wettbewerb
unjust enrichment	Ungerechtfertigte Bereicherung

c) Erläuterung der Fachterminologie

Da sich das Recht in verschiedenen Rechtssystemen unterschiedlich entwickelt hat, sind auch die Bezeichnungen der Rechtsgebiete unterschiedlich. Das *law of obligations* z.B. ist in dieser Form dem *common law* fremd. Diese Bezeichnung wird im Englischen eher verwendet, wenn man sich z.B. auf das deutsche Schuldrecht bezieht, das sowohl die vertraglichen als auch die gesetzlichen Schuldverhältnisse umfasst. Im *common law* ist das Schuldrecht aufgeteilt in *contracts*, *torts*, *unjust enrichment* etc.

Beim Arbeitsrecht muss unterschieden werden zwischen Individualarbeitsrecht (*employment law*) und dem kollektiven Arbeitsrecht (*labor law* – AE; *labour law* – BE).

Das **Erbrecht** kann im Englischen mehrere Entsprechungen haben: *law of succession*, *inheritance law* oder *wills and trusts*. Da sich im *common law* das Erbrecht grundlegend von dem im *civil law* unterscheidet, sind Fragen, die wir im deutschen Recht dem Erbrecht zuordnen würden, im *common law* bisweilen in anderen Rechtsgebieten, z.B. dem *property* zu finden.

Das große Rechtsgebiet des *commercial law* hat wiederum im deutschen Recht keine Entsprechung. Hierin enthalten sind Fragen, die wir dem Handelsrecht, dem Kreditsicherungsrecht oder dem Kaufvertragsrecht zuordnen würden.

In Südafrika und Namibia wird das Deliktsrecht nicht *torts*, sondern *delict* genannt.

Letztendlich können die Begriffe *conflict of laws* und *private international law* für Unklarheit sorgen. *Conflict of laws* ist enger zu verstehen, meint meist nur das Kollisionsrecht, wohingegen *private international law* sich auch auf Fragen der internationalen Zuständigkeit und der Anerkennung und Vollstreckung von ausländischen Entscheidungen beziehen kann. *Conflict of laws* wird in den USA verwendet, *private international law* eher im Vereinigten Königreich.

In juristischen Texten werden die **Rechtsgebiete häufig groß geschrieben**.

d) Lernkontrolle

Bitte ergänzen Sie die englischen Begriffe:

aufgrund, wegen   _____

Deliktsrecht (2×)   a) _____ b) _____

Entsprechung, Pendant   _____

Erbrecht (2×)   a) _____

                b) _____

Europäisches Gemeinschaftsrecht _____

Gesellschaftsrecht   _____

(Individual-)Arbeitsrecht   _____

Internationales Privatrecht (2×) a) _____

                                  b) _____

Kartellrecht   _____

Kollektives Arbeitsrecht   _____

Öffentliches Recht   _____

Patentrecht   _____

Privatrecht   _____

Rechtsgeschichte   _____

Rechtsvergleichung   _____

Sachenrecht   _____

Schuldrecht   _____

Steuerrecht   _____

Strafprozessrecht   _____

Strafrecht   _____

Umweltrecht   _____

Ungerechtfertigte Bereicherung   _____

Unlauterer Wettbewerb   _____

Urheberrecht   _____

Verfassungsrecht   _____

Verwaltungsrecht   _____

Völkerrecht   _____

Wirtschaftsrecht   _____

Zivilprozessrecht   _____

Lösung siehe S. 117

III. Development of US Law

a) Text

1. The Founding Fathers: The United States as it exists today was founded in 1789, when its Constitution entered into effect. The history of its law, however, goes back much further in time. In 1607, the first settlers reached Jamestown, Virginia. Others quickly followed and settled along the East Coast, the most famous being the Pilgrims, who sailed to America on the Mayflower. The Pilgrims fled Europe because they had not been permitted to freely exercise their religion. Indeed, the vast majority of immigrants to the New World had been persecuted in their native countries for political or religious reasons. Many also fled unemployment and poverty. Based on this history freedom of religion, freedom of speech and the pursuit of happiness (implying a certain degree of wealth) were of great importance to the founders of the new country and became the cornerstones of the *Declaration of Independence* in 1776 and the *Bill of Rights* in 1791.

2. Roots of US Law: US law has its roots in the English common law system. Common law is not created by scholars, but instead by practitioners, who develop it case-by-case. As the US began to develop, it became clear that legislative acts being passed by a legislative body that had not even been elected, would have taken much too long. Thus, it was preferable to apply English cases to US controversies than it was to apply no law during the years it would have taken to pass legislation. Therefore, even after declaring independence from England, the new states, with one exception (Louisiana), continued to apply English law. Louisiana, however, created a civil code modelled on the French *Code civil*. To this day, Louisiana's legal system follows the civil law legal tradition.

3. The U.S. Constitution: When signed in 1789, the U.S. Constitution did not provide for certain fundamental rights. Rather, its provisions focused on governing relations between the three different powers set forth therein: the legislature, the executive and the judiciary. The provisions of the U.S. Constitution correspond to the German *"Staatsorganisationsrecht"*. Immediately following the Constitution's entry into force in 1789, many influential politicians were not happy with the failure to include basic rights in the Constitution. Also motivated by the success of the French Revolution, the new Congress quickly passed the first 10 amendments, called *Bill of Rights*, containing what they considered to be the most important basic human and civil rights, such as the freedom of religion, the freedom of speech, the right to bear arms, the freedom of peaceful assembly, the freedom of the press and the separation of church and state.

b) Vokabeln zum Text

apply, to	anwenden
Bill of Rights	*siehe unten*
consider, to	erachten
Constitution	Verfassung (*siehe unten*)
controversy	Streitigkeit (*siehe unten*)
cornerstone	Eckpfeiler
declare, to	erklären, eine Erklärung abgeben
Declaration of Independence	Unabhängigkeitserklärung
elect, to	wählen
enter into effect, to	in Kraft treten (*siehe unten*)
entry into force	Inkrafttreten
executive power	ausführende Gewalt
exercise a right, to	ein Recht ausüben
failure	Scheitern, Ausbleiben
founding fathers	Gründerväter
freedom of religion	Religionsfreiheit
freedom of speech	Redefreiheit
fundamental right	Grundrecht
govern, to	regieren
however	jedoch
immigrant	Einwanderer, Einwanderin
judiciary, judicial power	rechtsprechende Gewalt
law	*hier:* Recht
legislative act	Akt der Gesetzgebung
legislative body	gesetzgebendes Organ
legislature, legislative power	gesetzgebende Gewalt
pass an act, to	ein Gesetz erlassen, verabschieden
permit, to	erlauben
persecute, to	verfolgen
practitioner	Praktiker/in
preferable	vorzugswürdig
provide for, to	gewährleisten, bereitstellen, beinhalten
provision	Regelung, Norm, Bestimmung
relation	Beziehung
right to bear arms	Recht, Waffen zu tragen
root	Wurzel, Ursprung
scholar	Wissenschaftler, Gelehrter (*siehe Exkurs*)
separation	Trennung (*siehe unten*)
set forth, to	darlegen, vorschreiben
sign, to	unterzeichnen
therefore	daher
thus	daher

c) Erläuterung der Fachterminologie

Der Begriff *Constitution* wird regelmäßig groß geschrieben. Wird die US-amerikanische Verfassung geändert oder ergänzt, so fließt diese Änderung nicht in den Originaltext ein, wie dies z.B. bei der deutschen Verfassung der Fall ist. Es wird hingegen jede Änderung als Verfassungszusatz (*amendment*) jeweils hinten angestellt. Wenn in einem Text auf einen bestimmten Verfassungszusatz Bezug genommen wird, wird *Amendment* groß geschrieben (z.B. "*The 1st Amendment of the U.S. Constitution contains …*").

Die ersten zehn Verfassungszusätze zur US-amerikanischen Verfassung werden **Bill of Rights** genannt. Sie enthält eine Vielzahl von Freiheitsrechten, wie sie auch der Grundrechtskatalog des deutschen Grundgesetzes enthält.

Für „**in Kraft treten**" kommen im Englischen (mindestens) sechs Möglichkeiten in Betracht:
- to enter into force
- to come into force
- to enter into effect
- to come into effect
- to enter into operation
- to come into operation

Ebenfalls möglich ist *to become effective*. Das Inkrafttreten ist *entry into force*.

Die Begriffe *controversy* und *dispute* können weitgehend synonym verwendet werden. Dies gilt ebenso für *freedom* und *liberty*.

„**Ein Gesetz erlassen**" kann zum einen ausgedrückt werden mit *to pass a law* oder auch mit *to enact*.

Der deutsche Begriff „**wählen**" hat im Englischen zwei Entsprechungen, je nachdem, ob es inhaltlich um die Handlung (wählen im Sinne von seine Stimme abgeben) oder um den Bezug zu einer bestimmten zur Wahl stehenden Person (jemanden wählen) geht. Ersteres ist *to vote*, Letzteres *to elect*.

Die Schreibweise des Begriffs *separation* sollte man sich gut einprägen. Vor allem statt des ersten „a" wird häufig fälschlich „e" geschrieben.

d) Lernkontrolle

Bitte ergänzen Sie die englischen Begriffe:

Akt der Gesetzgebung	_____
anwenden	_____
ausführende Gewalt	_____
Beziehung	_____
daher (2×)	a) _____ b) _____
das Recht, Waffen zu tragen	_____
ein Gesetz erlassen (2×)	a) _____ b) _____
ein Recht ausüben	_____

Einwanderer, Einwanderin   _____

erachten   _____

erklären, eine E. abgeben   _____

erlauben   _____

Freiheit (2×)   a) _____ b) _____

jedoch   _____

Gesetz (3×)   a) _____ b) _____

                        c) _____

gesetzgebendes Organ   _____

gesetzgebende Gewalt   _____

gewährleisten, bereitstellen   _____

Grundrecht   _____

in Kraft treten (2×)   a) _____ b) _____

Inkrafttreten   _____

Praktiker/in   _____

rechtsprechende Gewalt   _____

Redefreiheit   _____

regeln   _____

Regelung, Norm, Bestimmung   _____

Religionsfreiheit   _____

Streitigkeit (2×)   a) _____ b) _____

Trennung von Kirche und Staat   _____

Unabhängigkeitserklärung   _____

unterzeichnen   _____

Ursprung, Wurzel   _____

Verfassung   _____

Verfassungszusatz   _____

verfolgen   _____

wählen (2×)   a) _____ b) _____

Wissenschaftler/in, Gelehrte(r)   _____

Lösung siehe S. 118

IV. Sources of Law

a) Text

Sources of law are similar in most legal systems. There are primary sources of law such as positive law, case law, and to a certain degree also customary law. Positive law can be created by parliament (legislative power) or by the government (executive power). Laws made by parliament are called statutes. A statute that has not been passed, but is discussed by parliament as a draft, is called a bill. In some areas of law, parliament may confer legislative power on the government. Laws made by the executive power are called regulations.

Certain areas of law in the common law tradition are not fully governed by statutes or regulations. Contract and tort law, for example, are both based almost entirely on case law. In common law legal systems, judicial decisions are of greater importance than in civil law countries. They are binding on lower courts. This is the principle of *stare decisis*. If a higher court has already rendered a decision in a particular case, lower courts in the same jurisdiction are bound by the higher court's decision. In Germany, however, a court of first instance may deviate from a decision of the *Bundesgerichtshof*, at least theoretically.

In common law, the decision of a court in one jurisdiction may even influence the outcome of a dispute before a court in another jurisdiction. Case law rendered by courts in a different jurisdiction is considered to be persuasive. Therefore, a court in one jurisdiction is free to follow the reasoning and holding of a decision rendered by a court in another jurisdiction, but it has no obligation to do so. Most common law courts, however, do at least take into consideration decisions in other jurisdictions. Each state of the United States has its own constitution. In addition, both positive law and case law exist on a federal and state level. As a result, there are fifty independent bodies of state law, in addition to the body of federal law created by Congress. Some areas of law are predominantly governed by federal law, such as antitrust and bankruptcy law, while other areas of law are reserved to the states, such as family law.

Besides the primary sources of law there are also secondary sources of law. Lawyers are not obliged to follow views expressed in secondary sources. Often, however, they are helpful to find a solution to a legal problem. This is why lawyers consult the so called doctrine, i.e. law review articles and views expressed by law school professors in treatises. Smaller treatises are called hornbooks. If someone practicing within the common law legal tradition has to find out about the interpretation of a certain legal term, he often looks it up in a dictionary or more specifically in a legal dictionary. The most famous legal dictionary in the US is "Black's Law Dictionary".

power	*source of law created*
legislative power	statutes
executive power	regulations
judicial power	case law

b) Vokabeln zum Text

antitrust (Law)	Kartellrecht
area of law	Rechtsgebiet
as a result	demzufolge, im Ergebnis
bankruptcy law	Insolvenzrecht
be considered, to	betrachtet werden
be governed by, to	geregelt sein durch
be obliged to, to	verpflichtet sein
be reserved to, to	vorbehalten sein
bill	Gesetzentwurf
binding	rechtsverbindlich
body of law	*siehe unten*
case law	Fallrecht, Rechtsprechung
confer, to	übertragen
consult, to	befragen, zu Rate ziehen
court of first instance	Gericht erster Instanz
create, to	erschaffen
customary law	Gewohnheitsrecht
deviate from, to	abweichen von
dispute	Streitigkeit
doctrine	Schrifttum, Literatur
draft	Entwurf
e.g. (exempli gratia)	z.B. (zum Beispiel)
entirely	völlig, gänzlich
express, to	ausdrücken, zum Ausdruck bringen
federal law	Bundesrecht
follow a view, to	einer Ansicht folgen
government	Regierung
holding	*siehe unten*
hornbook	Lehrbuch
i.e. (id est)	d.h. (das heißt)
interpretation	Auslegung (*siehe unten*)
judicial decision	Gerichtsentscheidung
jurisdiction	Gerichtsbezirk i.w.S.
law (review) article	juristischer Aufsatz
law review	juristische Zeitschrift (*siehe unten*)
lawyer	Jurist/in; Anwalt, Anwältin (*siehe unten*)
legal dictionary	Rechtswörterbuch
legal problem	rechtliches Problem
legal system	Rechtssystem
legislative power	Gesetzgebungsgewalt
lower court	unteres Gericht
obligation	Verpflichtung
outcome	Ergebnis
particular	besonders, speziell
persuasive	überzeugend

positive law	gesetztes Recht
predominantly	überwiegend
primary source of law	primäre Rechtsquelle
reasoning	Begründung
regulation	Verordnung
render a decision, to	eine Entscheidung erlassen
secondary source of law	sekundäre Rechtsquelle
source of law	Rechtsquelle
stare decisis	*siehe unten*
statute	Gesetz
take sth. into consideration, to	etwas in Betracht ziehen
to a certain degree	zu einem gewissen Grad
treatise	Lehrbuch
views	Ansichten

c) Erläuterung der Fachterminologie

Die Konzepte hinter den Begriffen *holding* und *stare decisis* sind Besonderheiten des *common law* und damit schwer in eine Rechtsprache des *civil law* zu übersetzen. Das *holding* ist der Teil eines Urteils, auf den die Entscheidung rechtlich begründet ist. Wenn zum Beispiel dem Kläger eines Rechtsstreits Schadensersatz zugesprochen wird, so sind die rechtlichen Begründungen dessen das *holding*.

Die Begriffe *decision* und *judgment* werden im rechtlichen Kontext weitgehend synonym verwendet, wobei *decision* weiter zu verstehen ist als *judgment*. Letzteres ist allein die Entscheidung, die vom Richter ausgesprochen wird. *Decision* ist allgemein „Entscheidung". Ist eine *Jury* in einem gerichtlichen Verfahren beteiligt, nennt man die Entscheidung der Jury *verdict*. Erst auf Grundlage des *verdict* erlässt der Richter sein *judgment*. Der Begriff für eine spezielle Entscheidung ist also eng geknüpft an die Person, bzw. das Gremium, das sie fällt. Da es im deutschen Recht keine *jury* gibt, sollte der Begriff *verdict* nicht übersetzt werden.

Lawyer ist ein Begriff, der häufig zu Unklarheiten führt. Er kann „Jurist" im Allgemeinen bedeuten oder „Anwalt" im Besonderen. *Interpretation* und *construction* sind Synonyme für „Interpretation". Ebenso *dispute* und *controversy* für „Streitigkeit". *Law review* und *law journal* sind beides Bezeichnungen für juristische Zeitschriften. *Draft* ist als allgemeiner Begriff für Entwurf, *bill* speziell Gesetzesentwurf.

Oft machen auch die **Abkürzungen** (*abbreviations*) in einer fremden Sprache Probleme: „i.e." steht für „id est", ausgesprochen „that is". Deutsches Pendant der Abkürzung ist „d.h." („das heißt"). Für „z.B." schreiben Sie im englischen „e.g." („exempli gratia") ausgesprochen „for example". Schreiben mehrere Autoren an einer Veröffentlichung, so wird bisweilen nur der erste genannt, gefolgt von „u.a." („und andere"). Dies entspricht im Englischen „et al." („et alteri"), ausgesprochen „*and others*". Möchte man auf einen Aufsatz verweisen, der mehrere Seiten umfasst, so schreibt man im Deutschen „ff." und im Englischen „*et seq*".

Dt. Abkürzung	ausgesprochen		Engl. abbreviation	spoken
d. h.	das heißt		i. e.	that is
ff.	folgende		et seq.	and the following
u. a.	und andere		et al.	and others
z. B.	zum Beispiel		e. g.	for example

d) Lernkontrolle Vokabeln

Bitte ergänzen Sie die englischen Begriffe:

Abkürzung   _____

Anwalt, Anwältin   _____

abweichen von   _____

Auslegung (2×)   a) _____ b) _____

Befugnisse auf jmd. übertragen   _____

Begründung   _____

d. h.   _____

demzufolge, im Ergebnis   _____

ein Urteil erlassen   _____

eine Ansicht zum Ausdruck bringen   _____

Entscheidung   _____

Entwurf   _____

etw. in einem Rechtswörterbuch nachschlagen   _____

Fallrecht, Rechtsprechung   _____

ff.   _____

geregelt sein durch   _____

Gerichtsbezirk i. w. S.   _____

Gesetzentwurf   _____

Gesetzgebungsgewalt   _____

Gewohnheitsrecht   _____

in Betracht ziehen   _____

Insolvenzrecht   _____

jemandem vorbehalten sein   _____

juristische Zeitschrift (2×)   a) _____ b) _____

juristischer Aufsatz   _____

Juryentscheidung   _____

Kartellrecht   _____

Lehrbuch (2×)   a) _____ b) _____

primäre Rechtsquelle   _____

Rechtsgebiet   _____

Rechtssystem   _____

Regierung   _____

Schrifttum, Literatur   _____

Streitigkeit (2×)   a) _____ b) _____

u. a.   _____

überwiegend   _____

überzeugend   _____

Urteil   _____

Verordnung   _____

verpflichtet sein, etwas zu tun   _____

Verpflichtung   _____

z. B.   _____

zu einem gewissen Grad   _____

Lösung siehe S. 119

V. Legal Education and Legal Professions

a) Text

To become a lawyer students in the US go to law school. They go there after the completion of college and study law for three years. The term "faculty" is used in the US to name all the professors teaching at law school. So "*Fakultät*" and "faculty" do not stand for the same thing. Students work for law firms during their law school summer break. During this internship they are called "summer associates". After graduating from law school, US lawyers do not go through a practical training period that is comparable to the German "*Referendariat*". Often, however, they get some training within the job they chose. In Namibia, e.g., a mandatory legal traineeship required in order to register for an exam to become a legal practitioner is called "attachment" or "practical legal training".

A lawyer can work as an associate at a law firm, as in-house counsel within a company, as a clerk at a court or as a notary. A clerk is an assistant to a judge. In-house counsels negotiate contracts for their company and represent it before court, if a legal dispute arises. Associate is the name of a lawyer working at a law firm before he eventually becomes a partner in that firm. People working as a "Rechtsanwalt" are called differently depending on the country in which they work. It is solicitor and barrister in England, advocate in Scotland, attorney in the US, attorney and advocate in South Africa, depending on the court they can appear before, and counsel and advocate in Namibia, again depending on the court they can appear before. Lawyers preparing the transfer of title for land are called conveyancers. From time to time some lawyers take on cases from clients who are too poor to pay the lawyer's fee. This is called "*pro bono*". Lawyers in the US charge their clients on the basis of contingency fees. This means that their fee depends on the outcome of the case. For example, if the client gets a high sum of damages, the lawyer will get between 30 and 50% of this sum. If the client loses the case, the lawyer will get nothing.

Similar differences can be seen at the court houses in different countries. Whereas in Germany judges can be rather young, a judge in England will have been a practitioner for decades before he will become a judge. Judges in the US are sometimes elected, sometimes appointed. The former do not have to have studied law. Here judges of higher courts are called "Justice". In Namibia, judges of Magistrates' courts are called "Magistrates". During a court trial judges and attorneys wear gowns. In criminal proceedings there are also public prosecutors bringing charges against the accused.

b) Vokabeln zum Text

accused	Angeschuldigte(r)
advocate	*entweder schottischer Anwalt oder südafrikanischer bzw. namibischer Anwalt, der die Zulassung zu einem höheren Gericht hat*
appoint, to	ernennen
arise, to	entstehen, aufkommen
associate	*angestellte Anwälte einer US-Kanzlei (siehe unten)*
attorney	*entweder US-amerikanischer Anwalt oder südafrikanischer Anwalt, der die Zulassung zu einem Gericht erster Instanz hat*
barrister	*englischer Anwalt, der den Mandanten vor Gericht vertritt*
bring charges against s. o., to	gegen jemanden Anklage erheben
charge, to	berechnen, in Rechnung stellen
clerk	*Assistent/in des Richters in den USA*
client	Mandant/in
company	Gesellschaft, Unternehmen
completion	Beendigung
conveyancer	*Urkundsperson bei der Übertragung des Eigentums an einem Grundstück*
counsel	*namibischer Anwalt, der die Zulassung zu einem Gericht erster Instanz hat*
criminal proceedings	Strafverfahren
damages	Schadensersatz
dispute	Streitigkeit
elect, to	wählen
fee	Gebühr
internship	Praktikum
issue, to	ausstellen
law firm	Kanzlei
law school	*entspricht der Juristischen Fakultät einer deutschen Universität (siehe unten)*
lawyer	Jurist/in, Anwalt, Anwältin
legal training	Praktikum
negotiate, to	verhandeln
notary	Notar/in
outcome	Ergebnis
partner	*Anwälte, die Teilhaber einer US-Kanzlei sind (siehe unten)*
public prosecutor	Staatsanwalt, Staatsanwältin
represent before court, to	vor Gericht vertreten
solicitor	*englischer Anwalt, der die gerichtliche Verhandlung vorbereitet, den Mandanten vor Gericht aber nicht vertritt*

study law, to	Jura studieren
summer associate	*Jurastudenten in den USA, die in den law-school-Ferien in einer Kanzlei arbeiten (siehe unten)*
the former	ersterer/e/es
transfer of title	Eigentumsübertragung

c) Erläuterung der Fachterminologie

Sowohl die juristische Ausbildung als auch die juristischen Berufe unterscheiden sich teilweise erheblich innerhalb der Rechtssysteme und vor allem zwischen *common law* und *civil law*. In den USA gehen angehende Juristen nach dem *college* für drei Jahre auf die *law school*. Dort ist das erste Jahr das mit Abstand wichtigste. Die Noten der *first year courses* entscheiden über die Aufnahme als *summer associate* in den Semesterferien zwischen dem ersten und dem zweiten Jahr. Die Auswahlverfahren für diese *summer internships* sind für deutsche Verhältnisse enorm aufwendig. Alle Kanzleien, die etwas auf sich halten, kommen zu den *law schools* und halten *interviews*, Vorstellungsgespräche. Bereits im Vorfeld werden hierfür Lebensläufe und Motivationsschreiben verschickt und gesichtet und Einladungen für ein Gespräch ausgesprochen. Häufig fällt die Entscheidung, ob ein Jurastudent nach seinem Studium an einer prestigeträchtigen Kanzlei beginnt, bereits nach dem ersten Jahr *law school*. Dort erwarten ihn beste Gehälter, aber auch Wochenarbeitszeiten von bis zu 90 Stunden. Ein Anwalt, der in einer Kanzlei als *associate* arbeitet, ist Angestellter und nicht auch Teilhaber an der Kanzlei selbst. Dies aber strebt jeder *associate* an, da damit nicht nur noch höhere *pay checks* erwartet werden können, sondern auch die Wochenarbeitszeit sinkt. Diese Möglichkeit des Aufstiegs zum *partner* rechtfertigt den großen Einsatz, der von den *associates* erwartet wird.

Die englischen Entsprechungen für den deutschen Begriff Rechtsanwalt unterscheiden sich je nach Land. Eine Auswahl dessen ist *attorney* für die USA, *barrister* und *solicitor* für England, *advocate* für Schottland, *attorney* und *advocate* für Südafrika und *counsel* und *advocate* in Namibia.

d) Lernkontrolle

Bitte ergänzen Sie die englischen Begriffe:

Angeschuldigte(r) _____

ausstellen _____

Beendigung _____

berechnen, in Rechnung stellen _____

Eigentumsübertragung _____

eine Streitigkeit entsteht _____

einen Mandanten vor Gericht vertreten _____

Ergebnis   _____

ernennen   _____

erstere/e/es   _____

Gebühr   _____

gegen jemanden Anklage erheben _____

Gesellschaft, Unternehmen   _____

Jura studieren   _____

Jurist/in, Anwalt, Anwältin   _____

Kanzlei   _____

Mandant/in   _____

Notar/in   _____

Praktikum   _____

Rechtsanwalt, Rechts-   a) _____   b) _____
anwältin (5×)
                             c) _____   d) _____

                             e) _____

Schadensersatz   _____

Staatsanwalt, Staatsanwältin   _____

Strafverfahren   _____

verhandeln   _____

wählen   _____

Lösung siehe S. 120

B. Constitutional Law

I. The U.S. Constitution

a) Text

On July 4, 1776, following the American Revolution, the former colonies in the New World cut ties with England and declared their independence. The "Constitutional Convention" that ultimately produced today's U.S. Constitution was held in Philadelphia in 1787. The Convention consisted of 55 delegates, representing a wide variety of interests and backgrounds. George Washington led the Convention, whose members were determined to protect liberty, establish justice and provide for their common defense.

In pursuing these objectives, the delegates agreed that the government's power should be separated into three branches: Legislature, Executive and Judiciary (separation of powers). According to Art. I of the U.S. Constitution all legislative power is vested in the U.S. Congress which consists of Senate and House of Representatives. The executive power is vested in the President (Art. II U.S. Const.), and the judicial power is vested in the U.S. Supreme Court. A system of checks and balances was created to prevent any single branch from becoming too powerful.

b) Vokabeln zum Text

according to	gemäß
checks and balances	*siehe unten*
consist of, to	bestehen aus
create, to	schaffen
cut ties with, to	Verbindungen abbrechen zu
declare, to	erklären
defense (AE), defence (BE)	Verteidigung (*siehe unten*)
delegate	Delegierte(r), Abgeordnete(r)
determined, to be	entschlossen sein
establish, to	gründen, schaffen
government	Regierung, *hier:* Staat (*siehe unten*)
hold a convention, to	eine Versammlung abhalten
independence	Unabhängigkeit
justice	Gerechtigkeit, *hier:* Rechtsstaat
liberty	Freiheit (*siehe unten*)
member	Mitglied
objective	Ziel

power	Macht, Befugnis
prevent, to	verhindern
protect, to	schützen
pursue, to	verfolgen
represent, to	vertreten
separate, to	trennen
separation of powers	Gewaltenteilung
ultimately	letztendlich, schließlich
vest power in someone, to	Befugnisse/Macht auf jemanden übertragen

c) Erläuterung der Fachterminologie

Der englische Begriff für „Verteidigung" wird im amerikanischen Englisch mit „s" (*defense*) und im britischen Englisch mit „c" (*defence*) geschrieben. Die Begriffe *liberty* und *freedom* sind annähernd synonym für Freiheit zu verwenden. *Liberty* hat eine Tendenz zur Spezialität in Richtung Bewegungsfreiheit.

Der Begriff *government* hat in den USA zwei Bedeutungen: Zum einen „Regierung" als ausführender Arm der Exekutive und zum anderen „Staat" im eher umgangssprachlichen Sinn. *Separation of powers* und *checks and balances* müssen im Zusammenhang betrachtet werden. Zum einen sind die drei Gewalten voneinander getrennt, zum anderen überwachen sie sich gegenseitig. Der Begriff *separation of powers* wird mit Gewaltenteilung übersetzt, der Begriff *checks and balances* hingegen bleibt regelmäßig **unübersetzt**.

	US	Germany
legislative power	Congress (Senate + House of Representatives)	Parlament (Bundestag + Bundesrat)
executive power	President	Kanzler/in (*Chancellor*)
judicial power	U.S. Supreme Court	Bundesverfassungsgericht

Synonym für *legislative power* ist *legislature*, Synonym für *judicial power* ist *judiciary*. Der englische Begriff für „Ziel" kann zum einen *objective* sein, wenn es sich um eher größere Ziele handelt, *goal*, wenn es eher kleinere Zielvorgaben sind.

d) Lernkontrolle

Bitte ergänzen Sie die englischen Begriffe:

bestehen aus   _____

Delegierte(r), Abgeordnete(r)   _____

eine Versammlung abhalten   _____

entschlossen sein   _____

erklären   _____

Freiheit (2×)   a) _____ b) _____

gemäß	_____
Gerechtigkeit	_____
Gewaltenteilung	_____
gründen, schaffen	_____
Kanzler/in	_____
letztendlich, schließlich	_____
Macht, Befugnis	_____
Macht übertragen an	_____
Mitglied	_____
Regierung	_____
schützen	_____
trennen	_____
Unabhängigkeit	_____
Verbindungen abbrechen zu	_____
verfolgen	_____
verhindern	_____
Verteidigung	_____
vertreten	_____
Ziel (2×)	a) _____ b) _____

Lösung siehe S. 122

II. The Bill of Rights

a) Text

Due to significant ideological conflict at the time, the Constitution of 1787 (that entered into force in 1789) did not address basic human rights. Over the course of the next two years, the demands for a statement that would guarantee certain basic human rights increased. When Congress met for the first time in 1789, James Madison proposed a set of amendments that would preserve and protect the rights and liberties of all citizens of the new country. Congress eventually approved a set of ten amendments, now known as the "Bill of Rights". The Bill of Rights came into force in 1791. It ensures fundamental rights, such as the freedom of speech or the freedom of religion. It also contains provisions regulating the rights of a person in criminal proceedings before court.

In the following, see Amendments I, II, and X of the Bill of Rights:

Amendment I: Congress shall make no law respecting an establishment of religion, or prohibiting the free exercise thereof; or abridging the freedom of speech, or of the press; or the right of the people peaceably to assemble, […].

Amendment II: A well regulated Militia, being necessary to the security of a free State, the right of the people to keep and bear Arms, shall not be infringed.

Amendment X: The powers not delegated to the United States by the Constitution, nor prohibited by it to the States, are reserved to the States respectively, or to the people.

b) Vokabeln zum Text

abridge, to	einschränken
address, to	*hier:* beinhalten
alter, to	verändern
amendment	*hier:* Verfassungszusatz (*siehe unten*)
approve, to	billigen, zustimmen
arms	Waffen
assemble, to	versammeln
basic right	Grundrecht
be entitled to, to	einen Anspruch haben auf
be reserved, to	vorbehalten sein
citizen	Bürger/in
criminal proceedings	Strafverfahren
delegate, to	delegieren, übertragen
demand	Forderung
due to	aufgrund

ensure, to	sichern, absichern, sicherstellen
establishment	Errichtung
free exercise	freie Ausübung
freedom	Freiheit (*siehe unten*)
freedom of religion	Religionsfreiheit
freedom of speech	Redefreiheit, Meinungsfreiheit
freedom of the press	Pressefreiheit
fundamental right	Grundrecht (*siehe unten*)
guarantee, to	garantieren
human right	Menschenrecht
in the following	im Folgenden
increase, to	ansteigen, sich erhöhen
infringe, to	verletzen
just	gerecht
law	*hier:* Gesetz
over the course of	im Verlauf von
peaceably	friedlich
people	Volk
powers	Befugnisse
preserve, to	bewahren
prohibit, to	verbieten
protect, to	schützen
provision	Regelung, Bestimmung
refuse, to	verweigern
regulate, to	regeln
respecting	in Beziehung auf, im Hinblick auf
respectively	beziehungsweise
shall not	darf nicht (*siehe unten*)
significant	bedeutend

c) Erläuterung der Fachterminologie

Zwei typische Stolperfallen der englischen Rechtssprache sind die Begriffe *shall* und *may*. Der unerfahrene deutsche Leser sieht in *shall* leicht ein *soll* und entnimmt damit der betreffenden Rechtsnorm fälschlicherweise einen Ermessensspielraum. *Shall* muss aber mit „ist" oder „muss" übersetzt werden!

> shall = muss
> shall not = darf nicht
>
> may = kann
> may not = darf nicht

May entspricht dem deutschen Rechtsbegriff „kann". In der negativen Version entsprechen *shall not* und *may not* dem deutschen „darf nicht".

Für den Begriff „**ein Recht verletzen**" gibt es im Englischen mehrere Übersetzungsmöglichkeiten: *to breach*, *to infringe* und *to violate*. *To breach* wird häufig im Vertragsrecht angewendet (*breach of contract*), *to infringe* häufig im *patent* und *copyright law* (*to infringe a patent*) und *to violate* im Verfassungsrecht, dem Strafrecht und dem Deliktsrecht (*to violate a duty of care*).

Problematisch ist auch die Fülle der Begriffe für „**Grundrechte**". Hier kommen in Betracht:

- basic rights
- human rights
- basic human rights
- fundamental rights
- civil rights

je nachdem, in welchem Kontext sie stehen. *Human rights* kann auch gleichgesetzt werden mit „**Menschenrechte**". *Civil rights* sind die Grundrechte, die aus der Bürgerrechtsbewegung in den USA der 1960er Jahre erwachsen sind. Damit kommt eine Übersetzung als „Bürgerrechte" in Betracht.

Der Begriff *amendment* wird nicht nur für Verfassungsänderungen bzw. **Verfassungszusätze** verwendet, sondern auch für Änderungen einfacher Gesetze. Er kann somit je nach Kontext auch mit „**Gesetzesänderung**" übersetzt werden.

d) Lernkontrolle

Bitte ergänzen Sie die englischen Begriffe:

ansteigen, sich erhöhen   _____

aufgrund   _____

bedeutend   _____

Befugnisse   _____

bewahren   _____

beziehungsweise   _____

ein Gesetz billigen   _____

Bürger/in   _____

Bürgerrechte   _____

darf nicht (2×)   a) _____ b) _____

delegieren, übertragen   _____

einen Anspruch haben auf   _____

einschränken   _____

Forderung   _____

freie Ausübung   _____

Freiheit   _____

friedlich   _____

ein Recht garantieren   _____

gerecht   _____

Gesetzesänderung _____

Grundrecht (2×) a) _____ b) _____

im Folgenden _____

in Beziehung auf, im Hinblick auf_____

kann _____

Menschenrechte _____

muss _____

Pressefreiheit _____

Redefreiheit _____

regeln _____

Regelung, Bestimmung _____

Religionsfreiheit _____

schützen _____

sichern, absichern, sicherstellen _____

Strafverfahren _____

verändern _____

verbieten _____

Verfassungszusatz _____

verletzen (3×) a) _____ b) _____

c) _____

versammeln _____

verweigern _____

Volk _____

vorbehalten sein _____

Lösung siehe S. 123

III. Further Amendments

a) Text

The Bill of Rights applied to all white men; however, it did not apply to the rest of the population. Certain groups of people, such as women, Native Americans and African-Americans, were not granted the same rights as white men. In addition, the Bill of Rights focused only on the protection of the individual against the federal government, and did not acknowledge that basic human rights could also be violated by the state. As a result, additional amendments to the Constitution were deemed necessary over the course of the next two centuries. In comparison to the German Constitution, relatively few changes have been made to the U.S. Constitution. In over 200 years, only 27 amendments (including the Bill of Rights) have been passed. Three important amendments were introduced after the Civil War (1861–1865): the 13th Amendment, which abolished slavery (1865); the 14th Amendment, which granted due process of law against the states and equal protection by the law (equal protection clause) regardless of sex (1868); and the 15th Amendment, which provided that all races could vote (1870). Women were given the right to vote in the 19th Amendment, ratified in 1920.

Amendments XIII to XV and XIX of the U.S. Constitution read as follows:

Amendment XIII: Neither slavery nor involuntary servitude, except as a punishment for crime whereof the party shall have been duly convicted, shall exist within the United States, or any place subject to their jurisdiction. [...]

Amendment XIV: [...]; nor shall any State deprive any person of life, liberty, or property, without due process of law; nor deny to any person within its jurisdiction the equal protection of the laws. [...]

Amendment XV: The right of citizens of the United States to vote shall not be denied or abridged by the United States or by any State on account of race, color, or previous condition of servitude. [...]

Amendment XIX: The right of citizens of the United States to vote shall not be denied or abridged by the United States or by any State on account of sex.

b) Vokabeln zum Text

abolish, to	abschaffen
abridge, to	einschränken
acknowledge, to	anerkennen (*siehe unten*)
apply to, to	anwendbar sein auf
as a result	demzufolge
be subject to something, to	etwas unterliegen
century	Jahrhundert

citizen	Bürger/in
civil war	Bürgerkrieg
deem, to	halten für, vermuten (*siehe unten*)
deny, to	verweigern, vorenthalten
deprive someone of sth., to	jemandem etwas entziehen, vorenthalten
due process of law	*siehe unten*
duly convicted	rechtmäßig verurteilt (*strafrechtlich*)
equal protection of the law	*siehe unten*
except	außer
focus on, to	sich konzentrieren auf
grant, to	zusprechen
however	jedoch
in addition	zusätzlich, darüber hinaus
in comparison to	im Vergleich zu
individual	einzelner
introduce, to	einführen
involuntary servitude	*hier:* unfreiwillige Dienste, Zwangsarbeit
jurisdiction	*hier:* Kompetenzbereich, Zuständigkeit
on account of	wegen
over the course of	im Verlauf von
population	Bevölkerung
protection	Schutz
provide that, to	vorsehen, dass/regeln, dass
ratify, to	ratifizieren
regardless of	ungeachtet
slavery	Sklaverei
violate, to	verletzen
vote, to	wählen
whereof	dessen

c) Erläuterung der Fachterminologie

„**Vermuten**" kann im Englischen auf mindestens drei Arten ausgedrückt werden: *to deem*, *to assume* und *to presume*. „Anerkennen" hat zwei Entsprechungen: *to acknowledge*, wenn es um die Anerkennung von Rechten geht, also eher materiell gesehen und *to recognize*, wenn es um die Anerkennung von gerichtlichen Entscheidungen u.ä. geht, also eher formell betrachtet. *Recognize* wird im amerikanischen Englisch mit „z" und im britischen Englisch mit „s" geschrieben.

To ratify (ratifizieren) hat wie im Deutschen auch im Englischen zwei Bedeutungen. Einmal für die Ratifizierung von Staatsverträgen auf völkerrechtlicher Ebene (Beispiel: *„an international treaty was ratified by Germany"*) und für die innerstaatliche Umsetzung von Recht durch den Erlass von Gesetzen (Beispiel: *„The German Bundestag has ratified a new Act on …"*).

Due process of law und *equal protection of the laws* des 14. Amendments der U.S. Verfassung sind wieder schwer zu übersetzen, da es sich um Konzepte des US-amerikanischen Rechts handelt. Am ehesten kann die *equal protection clause* mit „Gleichbehandlungsgrundsatz" übersetzt werden und entspricht auch am ehesten unserem Art. 3 Grundgesetz. Der *Due Process*-Grundsatz hat im Deutschen Recht kein Pendant und kann (darf) damit nicht übersetzt werden. Es handelt sich hier um eine Art Generalklausel, deren Inhalt durch *case law* des U.S. Supreme Court definiert wird. Aspekte der *Due Process Clause* entsprechen u. a. unserem Rechtsstaatsprinzip (auch *rule of law* genannt) und dem Grundsatz des fairen Verfahrens (*fair trial*).

d) Lernkontrolle

Bitte ergänzen Sie die englischen Begriffe:

anerkennen (2×)	a) _____ b) _____
abschaffen	_____
anwendbar sein auf	_____
Bevölkerung	_____
Bürgerkrieg	_____
demzufolge	_____
Der Staatsvertrag wurde ratifiziert.	_____
Die Sklaverei wurde abgeschafft.	_____
die Verfassung sieht vor, dass …	_____
ein neues Gesetz einführen	_____
ein Recht verletzen	_____
ein Recht zusprechen	_____
einschränken	_____
einzelner	_____
etwas unterliegen	_____
halten für, vermuten (3×)	a) _____ b) _____
	c) _____
Gleichbehandlungsgrundsatz	_____
im Vergleich zu	_____
im Verlauf	_____
Jahrhundert	_____
jedoch	_____
rechtmäßig verurteilt (*strafrechtlich*)	_____
Rechtsstaatsprinzip	_____
Schutz	_____

sich konzentrieren auf   _____

ungeachtet des Geschlechts   _____

verweigern, vorenthalten   _____

zusätzlich, darüber hinaus   _____

Lösung siehe S. 124

Abschnittstest Nr. 1

Für die Bearbeitung der folgenden Aufgaben haben Sie 60 Minuten Zeit.

1 **Please fill in the gaps using the words below**

> applied – binding – case law – common law – customary law – government
> – holding – judgment – obligation – parliament – persuasive authority –
> primary – reasoning – regulations – rendered – stare decisis – statutes

Sources of _____ legal systems are the same as

those in any civil law legal system. There is positive law which is either passed

by _____ – so called _____, or by the _____

_____ – so called _____. Beside positive law there

is also _____ which, based on the principle of _____

_____ , is _____ to lower

courts of the same jurisdiction. Case law _____ by

courts of another jurisdiction is considered to be _____

_____ . Following this concept there is no _____

for the court of jurisdiction A to follow the _____ and

the _____ of a _____ rendered

by a court in jurisdiction B. In addition to positive law and case law as

_____ sources of law there is, to a minor degree, also

_____ which can be _____ to a dispute.

2 | **Please translate into English**

Der Kongress darf kein Gesetz verabschieden, das die Gründung von Religionsgemeinschaften zum Gegenstand hat oder die freie Religionsausübung verbietet; oder die Meinungs-, oder Pressefreiheit; oder das Recht der Menschen, sich friedlich zu versammeln, einschränkt.

_____

_____

_____

_____

_____

_____

_____

_____

3 | **Please add the English equivalent**

abschaffen _____

abweichen _____

Angeschuldigte(r) _____

anwenden _____

Auslegung _____

Befugnisse/Macht übertragen _____

Begründung _____

das Recht, Waffen zu tragen _____

Deliktsrecht _____

Eigentumsübertragung _____

ein Gesetz erlassen, verabschieden _____

eine Entscheidung erlassen _____

einen Anspruch haben auf _____

einschränken _____

entstehen, aufkommen _____

Entwurf _____

Forderung _____

Gebühr _____

gemäß _____

Gesetz (3×)   a) _____ b) _____

                                     c) _____

Gesetzentwurf   _____

Gewerblicher Rechtsschutz   _____

Gewohnheitsrecht   _____

Grundrechte   _____

im Vergleich zu   _____

im Verlauf von   _____

Internationales Privatrecht   _____

Kartellrecht   _____

Mandant/in   _____

rechtmäßig verurteilt
(strafrechtlich)   _____

Rechtsvergleichung   _____

Regelung   _____

Schadensersatz   _____

stammen von, sich ableiten von   _____

überwiegend   _____

unlauterer Wettbewerb   _____

unterscheiden   _____

verfolgen   _____

verhandeln   _____

verweigern   _____

Völkerrecht   _____

vorsehen, dass/regeln, dass   _____

Ziel   _____

4 Please explain the three meanings (notions) of the term „common law" (in full sentences)

_____

_____

_____

_____

_____

_____

_____

_____

_____

_____

_____

_____

_____

_____

_____

5 Please translate into German

The United States, as it exists today, was founded in 1789, when its Constitution entered into effect. In 1620 the Pilgrims fled Europe because they had not been permitted to freely exercise their religion. As the US began to develop, it became clear that legislative acts, being passed by a legislative body that had not even been elected, would have taken much too long. Thus, it was preferable to apply English case law to US controversies than it was to apply no law during the years it would have taken to pass legislation. Therefore, even after declaring independence from England, the new states, with one exception (Louisiana), continued to apply English law. Louisiana, however, created a civil code modelled on the French _code civil_. To this day, Louisiana's legal system follows the civil law legal tradition.

_____

_____

_____

_____

_____

_____

_____

_____

_____

_____

_____

_____

_____

6 **Please fill in the four gaps underlined**

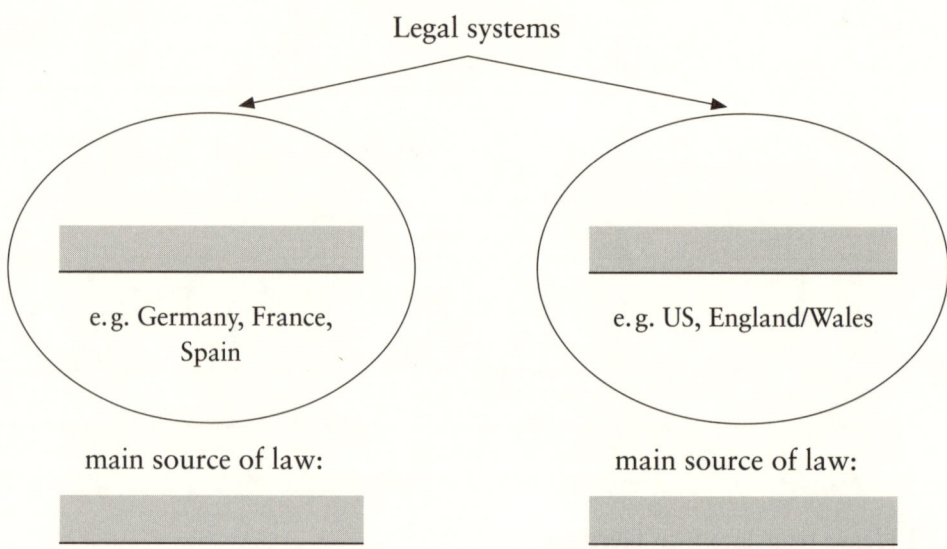

Legal systems

e.g. Germany, France, Spain

e.g. US, England/Wales

main source of law:

main source of law:

7 Bitte ordnen Sie die Rechtsgebiete soweit möglich dem Privatrecht oder dem Öffentlichen Recht zu und ergänzen Sie die deutsche Übersetzung. Orientieren Sie sich bei der Einordnung an der universitären Fächereinteilung der Vorlesungen

> *administrative law – antitrust – civil procedure – commercial law – company law – comparative law – conflict of laws – constitutional law – contracts – copyright law – criminal law – criminal procedure – criminology – E.C. law – employment law – environmental law – family law – intellectual property – labo(u)r law – law of obligations – law of succession – legal history – legal philosophy – patent law – property – public international law – tax law – torts – unfair competition – unjust enrichment*

Arbeitsrecht – Deliktsrecht – Erbrecht – Europäisches Gemeinschaftsrecht – Familienrecht – Gesellschaftsrecht – Gewerblicher Rechtsschutz – Internationales Privatrecht – Kartellrecht – Kollektives Arbeitsrecht – Kriminologie – Patentrecht – Rechtsgeschichte – Rechtsphilosophie – Rechtsvergleichung – Sachenrecht – Schuldrecht – Steuerrecht – Strafprozessrecht – Strafrecht – Umweltrecht – Ungerechtfertigte Bereicherung – Unlauterer Wettbewerb –

Urheberrecht – Verfassungsrecht – Vertragsrecht – Verwaltungsrecht – Völkerrecht – Wirtschaftsrecht – Zivilprozessrecht

Private Law		Public Law	
		Neutral	

8 **Please translate into English**

Neben den primären Rechtsquellen gibt es auch sekundäre Rechtsquellen. Juristen sind nicht verpflichtet, den Ansichten zu folgen, die in sekundären Rechtsquellen zum Ausdruck kommen. Häufig jedoch sind sie bei der Suche nach einer Lösung zu einem rechtlichen Problem hilfreich. Dies ist der Grund, warum Juristen das so genannte Schrifttum, d. h. juristische Aufsätze und Ansichten, die Juraprofessoren in Lehrbüchern zum Ausdruck bringen, zu Rate ziehen. Kleinere Lehrbücher werden *hornbooks* genannt. Wenn jemand, der innerhalb des *common law*-Rechtskreises arbeitet, etwas über die Auslegung eines bestimmten rechtlichen Begriffs herausfinden muss, schaut er häufig in einem Wörterbuch oder spezieller in einem Rechtswörterbuch nach. Das berühmteste Rechtswörterbuch in den USA ist *Black's Law Dictionary*.

_____
_____
_____
_____
_____
_____
_____
_____
_____
_____
_____
_____
_____
_____

9 Reading Comprehension: Please read Exkurs 1 on page 110/111 twice and explain in your own words where to be careful when translating legal texts from one language to the other and when it is safe to do so. Please give examples

_____
_____
_____
_____
_____
_____
_____
_____
_____
_____
_____
_____
_____
_____
_____
_____
_____

10 **Please fill in the gaps using the words below**

> *appear – assistant – associate – barrister – charge – clerk – clients – company – – contracts – conveyancers – country – court – damages – outcome – partner – solicitor*

A lawyer can work e.g. as an _____ at a law firm, as in-house counsel within a _____, as a _____ at a court or as a notary. A clerk is an _____ to a judge. In-house counsels negotiate _____ for their company and represent it before _____, if a legal dispute arises. Associate is the name for a lawyer working at a law firm before he eventually becomes a _____ in that firm. People working as a "Rechtsanwalt" are called differently, depending on the _____ in which they work. It is _____ and _____ in England, advocate in Scotland, attorney in the US, attorney and advocate in South Africa, depending on the court they can _____ before, and counsel and advocate in Namibia, again depending on the court they can appear before. Lawyers preparing the transfer of title for land are called _____. From time to time some lawyers take on cases from _____ who are too poor to pay the lawyer's fee. This is called *"pro bono"*. Lawyers in the US _____ their clients on the basis of contingency fees. This means that their fee depends on the _____ of the case. For example, if the client gets a high sum of _____, the lawyer will get between 30 and 50% of this sum. If the client loses the case, the lawyer will get nothing.

Lösungen auf S. 142

C. Criminal Law and Criminal Procedure

I. Crime, Offense and Misdemeanour

a) Text

The area of criminal law is what every non-lawyer seems to be most interested in. It provides a source for many novels and movies. Which one of the suspects committed the crime? What were his motives? Who was the victim? Minor crimes are called offenses, minor offenses are called misdemeanours. Most of the time the suspect is arrested after he has accomplished the crime. But even the attempt to commit a crime can be punished. In certain cases the suspect can be taken into custody and put into jail until the end of his trial, especially in serious and intentional crimes such as murder, rape or arson. A murder can be first-degree when it is committed in a particularly malicious way. Minor offenses are e.g. assault and battery, fraud, defamation or theft. A theft that is committed e.g. in a supermarket is called shoplifting and if a thief breaks into someone else's house in order to steal things it is called a burglary. If violence or intimidation is used against a person while the offender takes away the person's property it is called robbery. In his defense the suspect might allege that he acted in self-defense or defense of another, or that the victim consented to his conduct. Further, he may have acted in this certain way by mistake.

b) Vokabeln zum Text

accomplished	vollendet
act, to	handeln (*siehe unten*)
allege, to	behaupten
arrest someone, to	jemanden verhaften
arson	Brandstiftung
assault	Körperverletzung
attempt	Versuch
battery	Körperverletzung
burglary	Einbruchdiebstahl
commit, to	begehen
conduct	Verhalten
consent	Einwilligung
consent, to	einwilligen
crime	Straftat, Delikt, auch: Verbrechen
defamation	Beleidigung
defense of another	Nothilfe

first-degree	schwer (*siehe unten*)
fraud	Betrug
homicide	Mord (*siehe unten*)
in his defense	zu seiner Verteidigung
intentional	vorsätzlich, absichtlich
jail	Gefängnis (*siehe unten*)
malicious	böswillig, heimtückisch
manslaughter (*siehe unten*)	Totschlag
misdemeano(u)r	minderes Vergehen, Ordnungswidrigkeit (*siehe unten*)
mistake	Irrtum
murder	Mord (*siehe unten*)
non-lawyer	Nichtjurist/in
offender	Täter/in
offense (AE), offence (BE)	Vergehen; Delikt (*siehe unten*)
rape	Vergewaltigung
robbery	Raub
second-degree	mit bedingtem Vorsatz
self-defense (AE), self-defence (BE)	Notwehr
shoplifting	Ladendiebstahl
steal, to	stehlen
suspect	Tatverdächtige(r) (*siehe unten*)
take someone into custody, to	jemanden in Untersuchungshaft nehmen
theft	Diebstahl
thief	Dieb/in
trial	Gerichtsverhandlung
victim	Opfer
violence	Gewalt

c) Erläuterung der Fachterminologie

Grundlage einer Verhaftung, wenn nicht gerade auf frischer Tat ertappt (*to be caught red-handed* oder *to be caught in the act*), ist ein Haftbefehl (*arrest warrant*). Spricht man im Abstrakten vom „Täter", so benutzt man das englische *offender*. Sobald ein Tatverdächtiger (*suspect*) verurteilt und im Gefängnis untergebracht ist, wird er *convict* (Strafgefangener) genannt und nach seiner Freilassung spricht man von *felon*.

suspect ⟶ offender ⟶ convict ⟶ felon

Eine **schwere Tatbegehung** kann entweder mit *first-degree* ausgedrückt werden (bei Mord) oder mit vorangestelltem *aggravated* (z. B. *aggravated assault* = schwere Körperverletzung). Etwas komplizierter ist die englische Terminologie für die deutschen Bezeichnungen „Mord" und „Totschlag". Hier gibt es *murder*, entweder *first-degree* oder *second-degree* (mit bedingtem Vorsatz), *homicide* und *manslaughter*. Wird eine Person des öffentlichen Lebens ermordet, so kommt auch *assassination* (Attentat) in Betracht. Die Tatbegehung kann generell auch nach common law in aktives Tun (*act*) oder Unterlassen (*omission*) unterschieden werden.

Delikt	Täter	Handlung
arson	arsonist	to set on fire
assassination	assassin	to assassinate
assault	–	to assault
burglary	burglar	to burgle, to break in
defamation	–	to insult someone, to defame someone
fraud	fraud, defrauder	to deceive, to defraud
murder	murderer	to murder, to kill
rape	rapist	to rape someone
robbery	robber	to rob someone
shoplifting	shoplifter	to shoplift
theft	thief	to steal

d) Lernkontrolle

Bitte ergänzen Sie die englischen Begriffe:

anzünden, brandstiften _____

Attentat _____

Attentäter/in _____

begehen _____

Beleidigung _____

Betrug _____

betrügen (2×) a) _____ b) _____

böswillig, heimtückisch _____

Brandstiftung _____

Dieb/in _____

Diebstahl _____

einbrechen (2×) a) _____ b) _____

Einbrecher/in _____

Einbruchdiebstahl _____

Einwilligung _____

Gefängnis _____

Gerichtsverhandlung _____

Gewalt _____

Haftbefehl _____

handeln _____

Irrtum _____

jemanden in Untersuchungshaft
nehmen _____

jemanden verhaften/festnehmen _____

Körperverletzung (2×)   a) _____ b) _____

Ladendiebstahl _____

minderes Vergehen, Ordnungs-
widrigkeit _____

Mord mit bedingtem Vorsatz _____

Mord (2×)   a) _____ b) _____

Mörder/in _____

Nichtjurist/in _____

Nothilfe _____

Notwehr _____

Opfer _____

Raub _____

schwer (2×)   a) _____ b) _____

stehlen _____

Strafgefangene(r) _____

Straftat, Delikt, Verbrechen _____

Täter/in _____

Tatverdächtige(r) _____

Totschlag _____

Unterlassen _____

Vergehen, Delikt _____

Vergewaltigung _____

Verhalten _____

Versuch _____

vollendet _____

vorsätzlich, absichtlich _____

zu seiner Verteidigung _____

Lösung siehe S. 126

II. Who Are All These People in the Court Room?

a) Text

In the US, unlike in Germany, the judge plays a neutral role during the trial. Instead, it is the prosecutor (also called *district attorney* or *DA*) and the defense attorney who put forth the evidence and the arguments in an effort to achieve the most favorable outcome for their position. In a jury trial, the decision-making power is divided between the judge and the jury. The jury is composed of 12 people representing a cross section of society. The jury decides which allegations are based on sufficient evidence to become fact, and they apply the law as it is explained to them by the judge to those facts. A judge in the US does not have to be a lawyer. In many states, state court judges are elected by the people. In addition, witnesses may be either lay people or professionals. However, witnesses who appear before court in order to explain specific technical or medical data to the judge and the jury, are called expert witnesses. Unlike the German system, expert witnesses in the US are not appointed by court, rather they are chosen by each party.

b) Vokabeln zum Text

achieve the best outcome, to	das beste Ergebnis erzielen (*siehe unten*)
allegation	Behauptung (*siehe unten*)
appear before court, to	vor Gericht erscheinen
apply, to	anwenden
appoint, to	benennen
argument	Argument
be composed of, to	zusammengesetzt sein aus
cross section	Querschnitt
data (pl.)	Daten, Angaben
decision-making power	Entscheidungsbefugnis
defense attorney	Strafverteidiger/in
district attorney (DA)	Bezirksstaatsanwalt, Bezirksstaatsanwältin
divide, to	aufteilen
elect, to	wählen
evidence	Beweis (*siehe unten*)
fact	(erwiesene) Tatsache (*siehe unten*)
favo(u)rable	günstig
in addition	zusätzlich
in an effort to do sth.	in dem Bestreben, etw. zu tun
in order to	um zu
instead	stattdessen

judge	Richter/in
jury trial	Geschworenenverhandlung (*siehe unten*)
lawyer	*hier:* Jurist/in
lay people	Laien
outcome	Ergebnis (*siehe unten*)
party	Streitpartei
professionals	*hier:* Fachleute
prosecutor	Staatsanwalt, Staatsanwältin
put forth, to	vorbringen
represent, to	repräsentieren, vertreten
sufficient	ausreichend, hinreichend
trial	Verhandlung
witness	Zeuge, Zeugin

c) Erläuterung der Fachterminologie

Das Prinzip, das dem US-amerikanischen Strafprozess und vor allem der US-amerikanischen Verhandlung zugrunde liegt, ist das so genannte *adversarial system*. In Deutschland spricht man hingegen vom *inquisitorial system*. Je nachdem, welchem System eine Rechtsordnung im Strafprozess (und auch im Zivilprozess) folgt, unterscheidet sich die Rolle der Prozessbeteiligten. Der Richter im *adversarial system* ist recht inaktiv. Er leitet die Verhandlung, sorgt für Ruhe und trägt dafür Sorge, dass die Prozessregeln befolgt werden. Die Hauptarbeit im *adversarial*-Prozess liegt bei Staatsanwalt und Verteidiger. Beide sehen sich als Gegner. Der Staatsanwalt ist, anders als im deutschen Strafprozess, nicht neutrales Organ der Rechtspflege, sondern wird danach gemessen, wie viele Fälle er „gewinnt", wie viele Verfahren also mit einem Schuldspruch enden.

Weiterer Ausfluss des *adversarial system* ist der Umstand, dass nicht der Richter Zeugen und Sachverständige (*expert witnesses*) beruft, sondern generell die Parteien selbst.

In den USA hat jeder Angeklagte das verfassungsmäßig garantierte Recht auf eine Verhandlung vor einer Jury (*right to a jury trial*). Die Arbeitsteilung zwischen *jury* und Richter sieht vor, dass die *jury* die Behauptungen (*allegations*) der Parteien (Staatsanwalt und Verteidiger) daraufhin überprüft, ob sie hinreichend bewiesen worden sind (*sufficient evidence*). Ist dies der Fall, so werden sie als Tatsache (*fact*) behandelt. Der englische Begriff *fact* ist also spezieller als der deutsche Begriff „Tatsache", da sich im deutschen Prozess die Tatsache von der rechtlichen Darlegung abgrenzt, nicht aber danach, ob eine Behauptung bereits hinreichend bewiesen wurde.

Common law: allegation + sufficient evidence = fact

Achtung: *Evidence* hat im Englischen keinen Plural! Ein Synonym für *outcome* ist *result*.

d) Lernkontrolle

Bitte ergänzen Sie die englischen Begriffe:

Argument   _____

aufteilen   _____

hinreichende Beweise   _____

Behauptung   _____

Bezirksstaatsanwalt, -anwältin   _____

das beste Ergebnis erzielen   _____

Daten, Angaben   _____

eine(n) Sachverständige(n) benennen _____

Entscheidungsbefugnis   _____

Ergebnis (2×)   a) _____ b) _____

(erwiesene) Tatsache   _____

Fachleute   _____

Geschworenenverhandlung   _____

günstig   _____

in dem Bestreben, etw. zu tun   _____

Jurist/in   _____

Laien   _____

Querschnitt der Gesellschaft   _____

repräsentieren, vertreten   _____

Richter/in   _____

Staatsanwalt, Staatsanwältin   _____

stattdessen   _____

Strafverteidiger/in   _____

um zu   _____

Verhandlung   _____

vor Gericht erscheinen   _____

vorbringen   _____

Zeuge, Zeugin   _____

zusammengesetzt sein aus   _____

Lösung siehe S. 127

III. A Day in Court

a) Text

The bailiff walks the defendant to his seat. He is charged with first-degree murder. The 12 jurors watch his every move. The district attorney rises. He brought charges against the defendant two months ago and is now presenting his opening statement. He starts by reading the indictment to the defendant and the jury. After the DA's opening statement, the defense attorney presents his opening statement. Each party is focused on winning its case. The defense calls its first witness. Slowly the witness takes the stand. The defense attorney examines the witness. The district attorney then has the opportunity to cross-examine. The defense attorney has already prepared the witness for this situation. For days they have reviewed potential questions that the DA might pose. Nothing the DA asks should be a surprise to the witness. At the end of the trial, the judge explains the law to the jury and the jurors retreat for deliberations. Now it is up to the jury to decide whether the facts and the evidence are convincing enough to find the defendant guilty. They know he is presumed to be innocent. The defendant will only be found guilty if they all believe *beyond a reasonable doubt* that he has committed the crime.

Amendments of the U.S. Constitution with Reference to Criminal Procedure

Amendment VI: In all criminal prosecutions, the accused shall enjoy the right to a speedy and public trial, by an impartial jury of the State and district wherein the crime shall have been committed, which district shall have been previously ascertained by law, and to be informed of the nature and cause of the accusation; to be confronted with the witnesses against him; to have compulsory process for obtaining witnesses in his favour, and to have the Assistance of Counsel for his defence.

Amendment VIII: Excessive bail shall not be required, nor excessive fines imposed, nor cruel and unusual punishments inflicted.

b) Vokabeln zum Text

accusation	Anklagepunkt, Anschuldigung (*siehe unten*)
bail	Kaution, Sicherheitsleistung
bailiff	Gerichtsdiener/in
be charged with, to	etwas angeklagt sein
be confronted with, to	*hier:* gegenübergestellt werden
beyond a reasonable doubt	*siehe unten*
bring charges against, to	Anklage erheben gegen
call, to	aufrufen
commit a crime, to	ein Verbrechen begehen

compulsory	zwingend
convince, to	überzeugen
crime	Verbrechen
criminal prosecution	Strafverfolgung, *hier:* Strafverfahren
cross-examine, to	jmd. ins Kreuzverhör nehmen (*siehe unten*)
defense (AE), defence (BE)	Veteidigung
defendant	Angeklagte(r)
defense attorney	Strafverteidiger/in
deliberation	Beratung
district	Bezirk
enjoy a right, to	ein Recht genießen
examine, to	befragen, vernehmen
excessive	*hier:* unverhältnismäßig hoch
find someone guilty, to	jemanden für schuldig befinden
fine	Geldstrafe
impartial	unparteiisch
impose, to	auferlegen
in his favo(u)r	zu seinen Gunsten
indictment	Anklageschrift
inflict punishment, to	Strafe verhängen
juror	Geschworene(r)
murder	Mord
obtain, to	erwerben, erhalten
opening statement	Eröffnungsplädoyer
present, to	vortragen
presume, to	vermuten
previously ascertained by law	im Vorhinein gesetzlich bestimmt
require, to	fordern, erfordern
respectively	beziehungsweise
retreat, to	sich zurückziehen
review, to	*hier:* besprechen, immer wieder durchgehen
rise, to	sich erheben
speedy and public trial	zügige und öffentliche Verhandlung
take the stand, to	den Zeugenstand betreten
with reference to	mit Bezug zu

c) Erläuterung der Fachterminologie

Die Terminologie zu den deutschen Begriffen „anklagen", „Anklageschrift" etc. erscheint im Englischen anfänglich etwas kompliziert. Man muss genau zwischen materiellem und prozessualem Bezug unterscheiden:

Formell:

anklagen	= to bring charges against	(aus Sicht des Staatsanwalts)
angeklagt werden	= to be charged with	(aus Sicht des Angeschuldigten)
Anklageschrift	= indictment	

Materiell:

anklagen   = to accuse
Anklagepunkt   = accusation

Da wie bereits erwähnt im Strafverfahren der USA die Entscheidungsgewalt zwischen Jury und Richter aufgeteilt ist, muss auch terminologisch genau unterschieden werden. Der Schuldspruch der Jury wird *verdict* genannt, das Urteil des Richters auf dieser Grundlage ist dann das *judgment*.

„Angeklagter" kann im Englischen entweder *defendant* oder *accused* heißen.

Beyond a reasonable doubt ist die Formel für den Beweismaßstab in Strafsachen. Die Geschworenen müssen also über jeden vernünftigen Zweifel hinaus von der Schuld des Angeklagten überzeugt sein, um ihn schuldig zu sprechen. In Zivilsachen (*civil actions*) lautet die Formel: *the preponderance of evidence* muss für den Kläger sprechen, um der Klage stattzugeben.

Strafsachen	beyond a reasonable doubt
Zivilsachen	the preponderance of evidence

Die *cross-examination* (wörtlich „Kreuz-Befragung") ist ein weiteres für das *common law* typisches Rechtsinstrument. Es geht ebenfalls zurück auf das bereits angesprochene *adversarial system*. Beide Parteien, sei es im Strafverfahren oder in Zivilsachen, benennen „ihre" Zeugen (*witnesses*) und Sachverständigen (*expert witnesses*). Die Partei, die den Zeugen benannt hat, hat das Recht, ihn zuerst zu befragen. Da die Antworten des „eigenen" Zeugen in den allermeisten Fällen recht günstig für die eigene Seite ausfallen werden, hat auch die andere Seite das Recht, den gegnerischen Zeugen zu befragen. Skizziert man dieses Verfahren, so entsteht ein Kreuz.

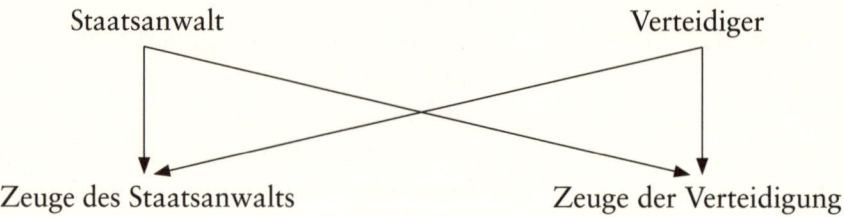

d) Lernkontrolle

Bitte ergänzen Sie die englischen Begriffe:

Angeklagte(r) (2×)   a) _____ b) _____

Anklage erheben gegen   _____

Anklageschrift   _____

Anklagepunkt, Anschuldigung   _____

etwas auferlegen   _____

einen Zeugen aufrufen   _____

jemanden für schuldig befinden   _____

einen Zeugen befragen   _____

Beratung _____

ein Eröffnungsplädoyer vortragen _____

etwas besprechen, immer wieder
durchgehen _____

beziehungsweise _____

Bezirk _____

den Zeugenstand betreten _____

ein Recht genießen _____

ein Verbrechen begehen _____

erwerben, erhalten _____

wegen etwas angeklagt sein _____

fordern, erfordern _____

gegenübergestellt werden _____

Geldstrafe _____

Gerichtsdiener/in _____

Geschworene(r) _____

im Vorhinein gesetzlich bestimmt _____

jmd. für schuldig befinden _____

jmd. ins Kreuzverhör nehmen _____

Kaution, Sicherheitsleistung _____

mit Bezug zu _____

Mord _____

Schuldspruch der Jury _____

sich erheben _____

sich zurückziehen _____

Strafe verhängen _____

Strafverfolgung, Strafverfahren _____

Strafverteidiger/in _____

über jeden vernünftigen Zweifel
hinaus _____

überzeugen _____

unparteiisch _____

unverhältnismäßig hoch _____

Verbrechen _____

Verteidigung

zu seinen Gunsten

zügige und öffentliche
Verhandlung

zwingend

Lösung siehe S. 128

D. Contracts, Sales Law and Secured Transactions

I. Contracts

a) Text

Contracts underlie many aspects of life. For example, landlords and tenants agree on the tenant living in the landlord's house in exchange for a monthly rent, sellers agree with buyers on a sale of goods in exchange for a purchase price, employers and employees agree on the latter performing services for the former in exchange for a salary, and lenders lend money to borrowers in exchange for additional interest to the back-payment of the money. The legal basis of these agreements is a contract: the lease, the sales contract, the employment contract and the loan. A contract requires an offer and an acceptance. Unlike in German law, in the common law a contract also requires "consideration." Consideration is the value that each party supplies to the transaction – the benefit each party confers on the other. Thus, in the common law a gift is not a contract because only one party supplies something of value to the other. Also, an assignment is not a contract, because only the assignor assigns receivables to the assignee. There are certain instances in which contracts can only be made in writing (not orally), for example, contracts for the sale of land must be in writing. In addition, contracts can be concluded in an express or an implied way. In an implied contract, the parties' intent to enter into a contract is assumed from the circumstances of the transaction.

b) Vokabeln zum Text

acceptance	Annahme
agree on, to	sich einigen über
agreement	Einigung, Vereinbarung
assignee	Zessionar/in
assignment	Abtretung
assignor	Zedent/in
back-payment	Rückzahlung
benefit	Nutzen
borrower	Darlehensnehmer/in
both ... and	sowohl ... als auch
buyer	Käufer/in
circumstances	Umstände
conclude a contract, to	einen Vertrag schließen (*siehe unten*)
confer on, to	jmd. etwas übertragen

consideration	*siehe unten*
contract	Vertrag
contract for the sale of land	Grundstückskaufvertrag
employee	Arbeitnehmer/in
employer	Arbeitgeber/in
employment contract	Arbeitsvertrag
enter into a contract, to	einen Vertrag schließen (*siehe unten*)
express	ausdrücklich
former	erstgenannter/e/es
gift	Schenkung
goods	Waren
implied	konkludent, stillschweigend
in addition	zusätzlich
in writing	schriftlich
instance	Fall, Umstand
intent	Wille, Absicht
interest	Zinsen
landlord, landlady	Vermieter/in
latter	letztgenannte
lease	Mietvertrag
legal basis	Rechtsgrundlagr/e/es
lender	Darlehensgeber/in
loan	Darlehen
offer	Angebot
orally	mündlich
party	Vertragspartei
purchase price	Kaufpreis
receivable	Forderung (*siehe unten*)
rent	Miete
require, to	benötigen, erfordern
salary	Gehalt
sale	Verkauf (*siehe unten*)
sales contract	Kaufvertrag
seller	Verkäufer/in
supply, to	einbringen, beitragen
tenant	Mieter/in
thus	daher, deshalb
to assume	vermuten
transaction	Geschäft
underlie, to	zugrunde liegen
unlike	im Gegensatz zu
value	Wert

c) Erläuterung der Fachterminologie

„Einen Vertrag schließen" kann im Englischen auf dreierlei Weise ausgedrückt werden:
- *to enter into a contract*
- *to conclude a contract*
- *to make a contract*

Einwendungen gegen die Wirksamkeit eines Vertrag (*defenses*) sind zum Beispiel:
- *misrepresentation* (Falschbehauptung)
- *fraud* (Täuschung)
- *duress* (Zwang, Nötigung zum Vertragsschluss)
- *undue influence* (das Ausnutzen von Schwäche oder Abhängigkeit einer Vertragspartei, vergleichbar mit § 138 BGB)
- *mistake* (Irrtum)
- *illegality* (Verstoß gegen ein Verbot, vergleichbar mit § 134 BGB)
- *public policy* (Verstoß gegen Gerechtigkeits- und Moralvorstellungen der Allgemeinheit, vergleichbar mit § 138 BGB).

Hierbei wird in den Wirkungen unterschieden, ob der Vertrag von Anfang an nichtig (*void*) oder der andere Vertragsteil lediglich zur Anfechtung berechtigt, der Vertrag also anfechtbar (*voidable*) ist.

Achtung: Die **Erfüllung** eines Vertrags (*specific performance*) ist im *common law* nicht die Regel, wie im deutschen Recht in § 362 I BGB verankert, sondern die Ausnahme. Grundsätzlich wird bei Nichterfüllung (*non-performance*) nur Schadensersatz (*damages*) gewährt. Die *specific performance* ist ein Rechtsinstitut der Equity.

Eine wesentliche Besonderheit des Vertragsrechts im *common law* ist das Konzept der **consideration**. Ein Versprechen (*promise*) ist nur dann Teil eines Vertrags, wenn damit ein Nachteil der versprechenden Partei verbunden ist. Der Vertrag muss also ein *bargain* darstellen, der andere Teil soll einen Nutzen (*benefit*) aus dem Geschäft ziehen können. Im *common law* gibt es daher keine einseitig verpflichtenden Verträge, wie z. B. im deutschen Recht die Schenkung.

Im Kaufrecht ist zu unterscheiden zwischen *sale* (Verkauf) und *purchase* (Kauf), wobei *sale* häufig als Synonym für „Kauf" verwendet wird.

Die allgemeinen Begriffe für Gläubiger und Schuldner heißen *creditor* (Gläubiger) und *debtor* (Schuldner). Im Arbeitsrecht kann das Entgelt für die Dienstleistungen entweder *salary* (Gehalt) oder *wages* (Lohn) sein.

Achtung:

Im common law gibt es **kein Trennungs- und Abstraktionsprinzip** (*principle of separation and abstraction*). Das heißt, dass hier das Eigentum an einer Kaufsache bereits mit dem Kaufvertrag und der Übergabe übergeht. Ein zweiter, dinglicher Vertrag ist nicht erforderlich.

d) Lernkontrolle

Bitte ergänzen Sie die englischen Begriffe:

Abtretung

Angebot

Annahme

Arbeitgeber/in

Arbeitnehmer/in

Arbeitsvertrag

ausdrücklich

benötigen, erfordern

daher, deshalb

Darlehen

Darlehensgeber/in

Darlehensnehmer/in

der Vertrag ist anfechtbar

einbringen, beitragen

einen Vertrag schließen (3×)   a)

                                    b)

                                    c)

Einigung, Vereinbarung

Einwendung

Erfüllung

erstgenannter/e/es

Fall, Umstand

Falschbehauptung

Forderung

Gehalt

Geschäft

Gläubiger/in

Grundstückskaufvertrag

im Gegensatz zu

Irrtum

jmd. etwas übertragen _____

Kauf _____

Käufer/in _____

Kaufpreis _____

Kaufvertrag _____

konkludent, stillschweigend _____

letztgenannter/e/es _____

Lohn _____

Miete _____

Mieter/in _____

Mietvertrag _____

mündlich _____

Nichterfüllung _____

nichtig _____

Nutzen _____

Rechtsgrundlage _____

Rückzahlung _____

Schadensersatz _____

Schenkung _____

schriftlich _____

Schuldner/in _____

sich einigen über _____

sowohl … als auch _____

Täuschung _____

Umstände des Falls _____

Verkauf _____

Verkäufer/in _____

Vermieter/in _____

vermuten _____

Versprechen _____

Vertrag _____

Vertragspartei _____

Waren _____

Wert   _____

Wille, Absicht   _____

Zedent/in   _____

Zessionar/in   _____

Zinsen   _____

zugrunde liegen   _____

zusätzlich   _____

Lösung siehe S. 130

II. Buying and Selling

a) Text

John and Jim have been friends for a long time. They are good business partners, too. John has set up his own little garage, where he not only repairs cars, but also sells certain spare parts. Jim is a wholesaler buying and selling car parts. One day John enters Jim's office.

John: Hey, Jim. How are you doing?

Jim: Hi, John! Fine. What can I do for you?

John: I need some winter tires. About ten sets. Is there something you can offer me?

Jim: Let's see ... How about these? Almost new, in excellent condition. I could give them to you for $80 per set. What do you think?

John has a close look at the tires and likes what he sees.

John: I think that's a fair deal.

John reaches out his hand, Jim takes it and by doing so they conclude a contract.

John: What if I discover some defective ones later? You know, I trust you, but you didn't get them right from the manufacturer either ... There's still warranty on them? Even though they are used?

Jim: That's right.

John: I'd need them pretty soon. When could you ship them?

Jim: I can deliver by tomorrow.

John: Great. Oh, ... and as to the purchase price ... can I buy them on credit? I can offer you a down payment of, say, $200, right away. The other instalments will follow.

Jim: Ok, but maybe you could pay another $100 on receipt of the goods?

John: Yeah, that's ok with me. So see you tomorrow.

Jim: Yes, see you.

John and Jim's contract was an individual one, concluded specifically between the two. However, often the seller already sets up contracts in writing before the buyer declares his interest. In these cases the seller often uses so called standard terms to ensure that it will be a good deal for him. It is in this way that he tries to maximize his profit.

The technical term for Jim's legal right deriving from John buying goods on credit is called "purchase money security interest" (PMSI). It is in its function equivalent to the German notion of "*Eigentumsvorbehalt*". It is a security interest in the sold goods specifically in order to secure the seller's risk should the buyer fail to pay the purchase price.

b) Vokabeln zum Text

as to ...	was ... betrifft
business partner	Geschäftspartner/in
buy, to	kaufen (*siehe unten*)
conclude a contract, to	einen Vertrag schließen
condition	Zustand
defective	fehlerhaft, mangelhaft
deliver, to	liefern (*siehe unten*)
discover, to	entdecken
down payment	Anzahlung
in writing	schriftlich
standard terms	Allgemeine Geschäftsbedingungen (*siehe unten*)
security interest	Sicherungsrecht
maximize, to	maximieren
ensure, to	sicherstellen
profit	Gewinn
instalment	Rate
manufacturer	Hersteller/in
offer, to	anbieten
on credit	auf Kredit
on receipt of the goods	bei Erhalt der Ware
purchase price	Kaufpreis
set up, to	aufbauen
ship, to	versenden, abschicken (*siehe unten*)
spare part	Ersatzteil
warranty	Gewährleistung(srecht)
wholesaler	Großhändler/in

c) Erläuterung der Fachterminologie

Bei der Frage, wie der Käufer in den Besitz der Waren kommt und welche Verpflichtung dabei der Verkäufer innehat, kann unterschieden werden zwischen *to ship* (versenden, abschicken) und *to deliver* (liefern). Ein Synonym für *standard terms* (Allgemeine Geschäftsbedingungen) ist *general terms and conditions*. Synonym für *to buy* ist *to purchase*. Verletzt eine Vertragspartei ihre aus dem Vertrag erwachsenden Pflichten, so spricht man von *breach of contract*.

Die englische Terminologie für die an der Lieferkette von Waren beteiligten Personen lautet *manufacturer* (Hersteller) – *wholesaler* (Großhändler) – *retailer* (Einzelhändler) – *customer* (Kunde).

manufacturer ⟶ wholesaler ⟶ retailer ⟶ customer

Synonym für *manufacturer* ist *producer*. Achtung: der *customer* (Kunde) kann leicht mit dem *consumer* (Verbraucher) verwechselt werden.

Das Rechtsgebiet Kreditsicherungsrecht lautet im Englischen *law of secured transactions*. Die Basis für ein Sicherungsgeschäft ist der Sicherungsvertrag (*security agreement*), im Deutschen auch Sicherungsabrede genannt. Sicherungsgut heißt *collateral*.

d) Lernkontrolle

Bitte ergänzen Sie die englischen Begriffe:

Allgemeine Geschäfts- bedingungen (2×)	a) _____	b) _____
Anzahlung	_____	
bei Erhalt der Ware	_____	
Einzelhändler/in	_____	
Ersatzteil	_____	
etwas auf Kredit kaufen	_____	
fehlerhaft, mangelhaft	_____	
Geschäftspartner/in	_____	
Gewährleistung(srecht)	_____	
Gewinn	_____	
Großhändler/in	_____	
Hersteller/in (2×)	a) _____	b) _____
kaufen (2×)	a) _____	b) _____
Kaufpreis	_____	
Kreditsicherungsrecht	_____	
Kunde, Kundin	_____	
liefern	_____	
maximieren	_____	
Rate	_____	
schicken, versenden	_____	
schriftlich	_____	
sicherstellen	_____	
Sicherungsgut	_____	
Sicherungsrecht	_____	
Sicherungsvertrag	_____	
Verbraucher/in	_____	
Vertragsverletzung	_____	
was … betrifft	_____	
Zustand der Waren	_____	

Lösung siehe S. 132

E. Torts and Damages

a) Text

The law of torts is one of the most important areas of law in practice. Every day hundreds of traffic accidents occur, doctors are sued for medical malpractice and companies are held liable for their defective products. In German law the most important legal basis for a tort action is § 823 subsec. 1 German Civil Code (*Bürgerliches Gesetzbuch* – BGB). It provides that a person who intentionally or negligently injures the life, body, health, freedom, property, or other right of another person unlawfully can be held liable for the harm caused.

Torts in common law are divided into many different groups like e. g. nuisance, trespass, or negligence. Some torts require some sort of fault: intention or negligence. Some torts belong to the group of strict liability. If the defendant of a tort claim wants to raise defenses he could bring forward that the plaintiff gave consent to his actions, that he acted in self-defense or that there was contributory negligence. In fact, tort law is quite similar to criminal law. It is the civil wrong aspect of an action that can also be punished by means of criminal law.

Lawyers often not only sue for compensatory damages (including damages for pain and suffering), but also for punitive damages. Punitive damages are a means of US law to punish the tortfeasor for the wrong he has committed and as an example to others, to keep them from committing a malicious and particularly fraudulent act like that. So punitive damages are a means of punishment and deterrence.

b) Vokabeln zum Text

be held liable, to	haftbar gemacht werden
be sued for, to	verklagt werden wegen
by means of	mittels
commit, to	begehen, verüben
company	Unternehmen, Gesellschaft
compensatory damages	kompensatorischer Schadensersatz
consent	Einwilligung
contributory negligence	Mitverschulden
damages for pain and suffering	Schmerzensgeld
defective product	fehlerhaftes Produkt
defendant	Beklagte(r)
defense (AE), defence (BE)	Einwendung, Einrede
deterrence	Abschreckung
fault	Verschulden
fraudulent	arglistig, betrügerisch

in practice	in der Praxis
intention	Vorsatz, Absicht
legal basis	rechtliche Grundlage
malicious	böswillig, heimtückisch
malpractice	*siehe unten*
means	Mittel
negligence	Fahrlässigkeit (*siehe unten*)
nuisance	Besitzstörung
occur, to	geschehen, sich ereignen
particular	besonders
plaintiff	Kläger/in
provide, to	bestimmen
punishment	Strafe, Bestrafung
punitive damages	Strafschadensersatz (*oder unübersetzt*)
raise, to	erheben
self-defense (AE), self-defence (BE)	Notwehr
slander	Verleumdung
strict liability	Gefährdungshaftung
subsection	Absatz
tort action	Klage aus unerlaubter Handlung
tortfeasor	Schädiger/in
trespass	Besitzstörung
wrong	Unrecht

c) Erläuterung der Fachterminologie

Das *law of torts* im *common law* ist extrem fallrechtsorientiert. Es gibt nur wenige gesetzliche Regelungen. Die einzelnen Voraussetzungen für einen Schadensersatzanspruch müssen im Wesentlichen einzelnen Fällen entnommen werden. Allerdings haben sich dabei Fallgruppen herausgebildet, die die Orientierung etwas erleichtern. Es gibt auch im *common law* verschuldensabhängige (*fault-based liability*) und verschuldensunabhängige Haftung (*strict liability*) für eine unerlaubte Handlung. Erstere differenziert ferner zwischen vorsätzlich (*intentional*) und fahrlässig (*negligent*). Deutsches Synonym für verschuldensunabhängige Haftung ist „Gefährdungshaftung".

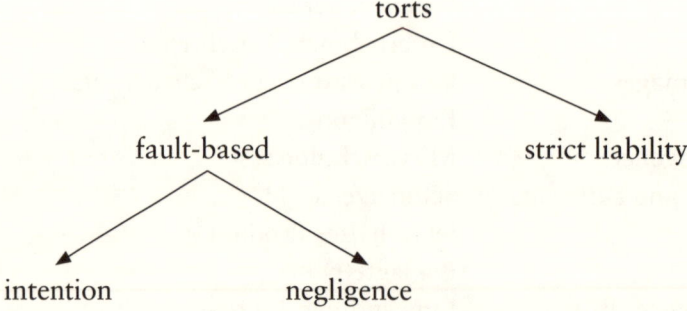

Das *common law* unterscheidet nicht wie das deutsche Recht im Tatbestand eines *tort* zwischen Handlung, Rechtsgutsverletzung und Schaden. Folgende Begriffe nähern sich diesen deutschen Begriffen aber an: *act* für Handlung (= aktives Tun und Unterlassen), *harm* oder *injury* für Verletzung, allerdings auch Synonym für Schaden, *damage* für Schaden und *damages* für Schadensersatz. Wichtig ist, dass *damage* im Sinne von „Schaden" im Englischen keinen Plural kennt, also bei der Übersetzung des deutschen Begriffs „Schäden" kein „s" am Ende stehen darf, da es sonst „Schadensersatz" bedeutet.

act ————————▶ harm ————————▶ damage ————————▶ damages
                      injury

Häufig entsteht Unsicherheit, wenn **deutsche Abkürzungen für Gesetzte im Englischen** zitiert werden sollen. Hier kann man nicht einfach die bekannten Buchstaben („BGB") heranziehen, da es sich hierbei ja um die Abkürzung eines deutschen Begriffs handelt. Es gibt mehrere Möglichkeiten.

Als Vorschlag kann folgende Regel dienen:

1. die englische Übersetzung der deutschen langen Gesetzesbezeichnung,
2. in Klammern die deutsche Bezeichnung des Gesetzes sowie
3. ebenfalls in der Klammer und mit Bindestrich angefügt die übliche deutsche Abkürzung.

Beispiel: German Civil Code (Bürgerliches Gesetzbuch – BGB)

d) Lernkontrolle

Bitte ergänzen Sie die englischen Begriffe:

Abschreckung   _____

arglistig, betrügerisch   _____

begehen, verüben   _____

Beklagte(r)   _____

Besitzstörung   _____

böswillig, heimtückisch   _____

Einwendung, Einrede   _____

Einwilligung   _____

fahrlässig   _____

Fahrlässigkeit   _____

fehlerhaftes Produkt   _____

Gefährdungshaftung   _____

geschehen, sich ereignen   _____

haftbar gemacht werden   _____

Klage aus unerlaubter Handlung   _____

Kläger/in   _____

kompensatorischer
Schadensersatz   _____

Mitverschulden   _____

Notwehr   _____

rechtliche Grundlage   _____

Schädiger/in   _____

Schmerzensgeld   _____

Strafe, Bestrafung   _____

Strafschadensersatz   _____

Unrecht   _____

Unternehmen, Gesellschaft   _____

verklagt werden wegen   _____

Verletzung (2×)   a) _____ b) _____

Verleumdung   _____

Verschulden   _____

Vorsatz, Absicht   _____

vorsätzlich   _____

Lösung siehe S. 134

Abschnittstest Nr. 2

Für die Bearbeitung der folgenden Aufgaben haben Sie 45 Minuten Zeit.

1 **Please translate into English**

Verträge sind die Grundlage für viele Aspekte des Lebens. So einigen sich zum Beispiel Vermieter und Mieter darüber, dass der Mieter im Austausch gegen den monatlichen Mietzins im Haus des Vermieters wohnt, der Verkäufer und der Käufer einigen sich über den Kauf von Waren im Austausch gegen einen Kaufpreis, Arbeitgeber und Arbeitnehmer einigen sich darüber, dass der Letztere Dienstleistungen gegenüber dem Ersteren im Austausch gegen Gehalt erbringt, und der Darlehensgeber leiht dem Darlehensnehmer Geld im Austausch gegen zusätzlich zur Rückzahlung anfallende Zinsen. Die rechtliche Grundlage für diese Einigungen ist ein Vertrag: der Mietvertrag, der Kaufvertrag, der Arbeitsvertrag und der Darlehensvertrag. Ein Vertrag erfordert sowohl ein Angebot als auch eine Annahme.

_____

_____

_____

_____

_____

_____

_____

_____

_____

_____

_____

_____

_____

_____

_____

_____

_____

2 **Please add the English equivalent**

Angeklagte(r)   _____

Anklage erheben gegen   _____

Anklageschrift   _____

Annahme   _____

auferlegen   _____

Behauptung   _____

Beleidigung   _____

Brandstiftung   _____

den Zeugenstand betreten   _____

der Vertrag ist nichtig   _____

Entscheidungsbefugnis   _____

Eröffnungsplädoyer   _____

fehlerhaftes Produkt   _____

Gerichtsverhandlung   _____

Gläubiger/in   _____

Hersteller/in   _____

jmd. verhaften   _____

jmd. etwas übertragen   _____

Kaufpreis   _____

Kaution, Sicherheitsleistung   _____

konkludent, stillschweigend   _____

Körperverletzung   _____

Kreditsicherungsrecht   _____

Kunde, Kundin   _____

Ladendiebstahl   _____

öffentliche Verhandlung   _____

Recht auf Verhandlung vor
einer jury   _____

Sachverständige(r)   _____

Schenkung   _____

schwere Körperverletzung   _____

Strafgefangene(r)   _____

unparteiisch	_____
Verhalten	_____
Vermieter/in	_____
Vertragserfüllung	_____
Vertragsverletzung	_____
vollendet	_____
zwingend	_____

3 **Please add the respective counterpart**

offer	–	_____
tenant	–	_____
express	–	_____
creditor	–	_____
in writing	–	_____
assignor	–	_____
borrower	–	_____
seller	–	_____
employer	–	_____
goods	–	_____

4 **Please fill in the gaps using the words below**

> _achieve – allegations – appear – appointed – DA – decision – defense attorney – elected – evidence – expert witnesses – explain – judge (2×) – jury – lawyer – prosecutor – representing – trial_

In the US, unlike in Germany, the _____ plays a neutral role during a trial. Instead, it is the _____ (also called "the district attorney" or "_____") and the _____ who put forth the _____ and the arguments in an effort to _____ the most favorable outcome for their position. In a jury_____, the _____-making power is divided between the judge and the jury. The jury is composed of 12 people _____ a cross section of society. The _____ decides which _____ are based on sufficient evidence to become fact, and they apply the law as it is explained to them by the _____ to those facts. A judge in the US does not have to be a _____ . In many states, state court judges are _____ by the people. Witnesses who _____ before court in order to _____ specific technical or medical data to the judge and the jury, are called _____ . Unlike the German system, expert witnesses in the US are not _____ by court, rather they are chosen by each party.

5 **Please add the respective English terminology**

	Delikt	Täter	Handlung
Brandstiftung			
Attentat			
Körperverletzung		–	
Einbruchdiebstahl			
Beleidigung		–	
Betrug			
Mord			
Vergewaltigung			
Raub			
Ladendiebstahl			
Diebstahl			

6 **Please translate into German**

A murder can be first-degree when it is committed in a particularly malicious way. Minor offenses are e.g. assault and battery, fraud, defamation or theft. If a theft is committed in a supermarket it is called shoplifting and if the thief broke into someone else's house in order to steal things it becomes a burglary and if he uses violence or intimidation against a person while he takes away the person's property it is called robbery. In his defense the suspect might allege that he has acted in self-defense or defense of another, or that the victim has consented to his conduct. Also he might have acted in this certain way by mistake.

_____

_____

_____

_____

_____

_____

_____

_____

_____

_____

_____

_____

_____

7 **Please explain the term "cross-examination"**

_____

_____

_____

_____

_____

_____

_____

_____

_____

_____

_____

_____

_____

_____

Lösungen auf S. 149

F. Property

a) Text

Property law is closely linked to many other areas of law such as the law of contracts, the law of secured transactions, bankruptcy law or the law of inheritance. This link is even closer in common law legal systems than in German law because, unlike in German law, in most common law legal systems there is no principle of separation and abstraction which separates and distinguishes between two different kinds of contracts: those that lead to an obligation to transfer property, and those that actually transfer the property.

Things are divided into separate categories: There is movable property and immovable property. Movable property includes for example cars, clothes, chairs and tables, immovable property is used for pieces of land, also called real estate. Both movable and immovable property have synonyms: Movable property equals personal property, immovable property equals real property. Movable property might be tangible or intangible. Tangible movable property is called chattel. Examples for intangibles are patents and receivables.

The relationship a person has to a thing can be divided into possession and property. The possessor might gain or take possession, remain in possession, surrender and resume possession, and at the end he might finally relinquish possession if there was no dispossession of any kind before. If someone interferes with someone else's possession you call this trespass. Property has two synonyms: ownership and title. After the transfer of title the property passes from the old to the new owner, who can also be called proprietor. If the person transferring the title has not been the owner of the thing the title might pass nevertheless on the basis of a bona fide purchase. From the viewpoint of the buyer he is acquiring ownership, unless, according to German law, the seller has declared retention (also called reservation) of title.

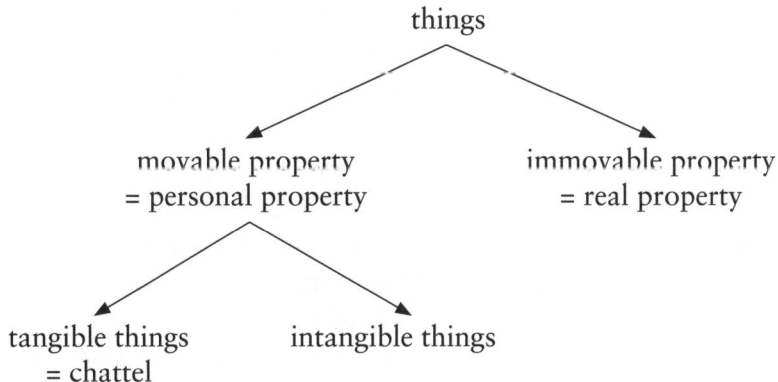

b) Vokabeln zum Text

acquire, to	erwerben
bona fide purchase	gutgläubiger Erwerb
chattel	körperliche Gegenstände
dispossession	Besitzentziehung
gain possession, to	Besitz erlangen
immovable property	unbewegliche Sachen
intangible property	unkörperliche Gegenstände
interfere with, to	stören, beeinträchtigen
law of secured transactions	Kreditsicherungsrecht
movable property	bewegliche Sachen
nevertheless	trotzdem, nichtsdestotrotz
obligation	Verpflichtung
owner	Eigentümer/in
ownership	Eigentum
passing of title	Eigentumsübergang
personal property	bewegliche Sachen
piece of land	Grundstück
possession	Besitz
possessor	Besitzer/in
principle of separation and abstraction	Trennungs- und Abstraktionsprinzip
property	Eigentum
proprietor	Eigentümer/in
real estate	Grundstück
real property	unbewegliche Sachen
receivable	Forderung
relinquish possession, to	Besitz aufgeben
remain in possession, to	in Besitz bleiben
reservation of title	Eigentumsvorbehalt
resume possession, to	Besitz wieder aufnehmen
retention of title	Eigentumsvorbehalt
surrender possession, to	Besitz aufgeben
synonym	Synonym
take possession, to	Besitz ergreifen
tangible property	körperliche Gegenstände
thing	Sache
title	Eigentum
transfer of title	Eigentumsübertragung
transfer property, to	Eigentum übertragen
trespass	Besitzstörung
unless	es sei denn
unlike	im Gegensatz zu, im Unterschied zu

c) Erläuterung der Fachterminologie

Auch das *common law* unterscheidet im Sachenrecht zwischen beweglichen und unbeweglichen Sachen. Es sind für beide jeweils zwei Bezeichnungen gebräuchlich:

Bewegliche Sachen:	movable property	personal property
Unbewegliche Sachen:	immovable property	real property

Property wird auch im Sinne von „Vermögen" verwendet. Die Gesamtheit der Vermögensgegenstände wird *assets* genannt. Wenn es um das Vermögen eines Verstorbenen, also seinen Nachlass, geht, so benutzt man im Englischen das Wort *estate*.

„Eigentum übertragen" hat im Englischen zwei Bezeichnungen, je nachdem, ob das Eigentum an beweglichen oder unbeweglichen Sachen übertragen wird.

Eigentum an beweglichen Sachen übertragen:	**to transfer title/property**
Eigentum an unbeweglichen Sachen übertragen:	**to convey**

Bei Letzterem kann verwiesen werden auf den **conveyancer** in der Einheit A.V. Legal Professions.

Auch im *common law* gibt es eine Eigentumsvermutung (*presumption of title*). Zur Sicherung können dingliche Sicherungsrechte (*security interests in property*) an Sachen übertragen werden. Auch kann das Eigentumsrecht beschränkt werden (*restriction of title*).

d) Lernkontrolle

Bitte ergänzen Sie die englischen Begriffe:

Besitz		_____
Besitz aufgeben (2×)	a)	_____
	b)	_____
Besitz ergreifen		_____
Besitz erlangen		_____
Besitz wieder aufnehmen		_____
Besitzentziehung		_____
Besitzer/in		_____
Besitzstörung		_____
bewegliche Sachen	a)	_____
	b)	_____
Eigent. an e. Grundstück übertragen		_____

Eigentum (3×) a) _____ b) _____

c) _____

Eigentum erwerben _____

Eigentümer/in (2×) a) _____ b) _____

Eigentumsübergang _____

Eigentumsübertragung a) _____
(an beweglichen Sachen) (2×)
b) _____

Eigentumsvermutung _____

Eigentumsvorbehalt (2×) a) _____

b) _____

Forderung _____

Grundstück (2×) a) _____ b) _____

Gutgläubiger Erwerb _____

in Besitz bleiben _____

körperliche Gegenstände (2×) a) _____ b) _____

Nachlass _____

Sache _____

stören, beeinträchtigen _____

Trennungs- und Abstraktionsprinzip _____

trotzdem, nichtsdestotrotz _____

unbewegliche Sachen a) _____

b) _____

unkörperliche Gegenstände _____

Vermögen (3×) a) _____ b) _____

c) _____

Lösung siehe S. 135

G. Family Law

a) Text

In the US, family law is governed by the states, rather than by the federal government. Family law in most jurisdictions encompasses at a minimum the law of marriage, termination of marriage, matrimonial property, financial support, custody of children and adoption. Marriages can be terminated either by an annulment or a divorce. An annulment means that the marriage was void or voidable from the start and, therefore, it is treated as though it never existed. A divorce, on the other hand, is a legal dissolution of the relationship of husband and wife. In most states, a divorce will be granted on the basis of adultery, desertion or cruel treatment, among other things. A "no-fault" divorce will be granted if the parties agree to terminate the marriage due to irreconcilable differences. In some cases, the court will award alimony to one spouse – the money paid for the maintenance of a spouse, for a definite or indefinite period of time. Similarly, if the couple has children, the court may decide to award custody and child support to one of the parties. In determining the custody of the children, the court must decide what is in "the best interest and welfare" of the children.

As to international family law, there is a wide number of international conventions that have to be taken into consideration before applying national law. Under the auspices of the Hague Conference on Private International Law, for example, many international agreements have been elaborated in this area:
- the Hague Convention concerning the Powers of Authorities and the Law Applicable in respect of the Protection of Minors (1961)
- the Hague Convention on the Law Applicable to Maintenance Obligations (1973)
- the Hague Convention on the Recognition and Enforcement of Decisions relating to Maintenance Obligations (1973)
- the Hague Convention on the Civil Aspects of International Child Abduction (1980)
- the Hague Convention on Protection of Children and Co-operation in respect of Intercountry Adoption (1993)
- the Hague Convention on Jurisdiction, Applicable Law, Recognition, Enforcement and Co-operation in respect of Parental Responsibility and Measures for the Protection of Children (1996).

b) Vokabeln zum Text

abduction	Entführung
adoption	Adoption
adultery	Ehebruch
alimony	Unterhalt(szahlungen) für den Ehegatten

annulment	Annullierung
apply, to	anwenden
auspice	Federführung, Schirmherrschaft
authority	Behörde
award, to	zusprechen
be governed by, to	geregelt sein durch
child support	Kindesunterhalt
custody	Sorgerecht
definite	begrenzt
desertion	Verlassen, Imstichlassen
dissolution	Auflösung
divorce	Scheidung
due to	auf Grund von
encompass, to	umfassen
enforcement	Vollstreckung
financial support	Unterhalt
grant, to	erteilen, zusprechen
husband	Ehemann
indefinite	unbegrenzt
international agreement	internationales Übereinkommen
international convention	internationale Konvention
irreconcilable	unüberbrückbare
jurisdiction	Zuständigkeit
maintenance	Lebensunterhalt, Unterhalt
maintenance obligation	Unterhaltsverpflichtung
marriage	Ehe
matrimonial property	ehelicher Güterstand
measure	Maßnahme
minor	Minderjährige(r)
parental responsibility	elterliche Verantwortung
recognition	Anerkennung
similarly	ähnlich
spouse	Ehegatte
take into consideration, to	in Betracht ziehen
termination of marriage	Beendigung der Ehe
the best interest and welfare of the child	Kindeswohl
therefore	daher
void	nichtig, ungültig
voidable	anfechtbar
wife	Ehefrau

c) Erläuterung der Fachterminologie

Der Begriff *alimony* ist der Unterhalt (*maintenance*) speziell für den geschiedenen Ehegatten. Der Unterhalt für das Kind wird im Englischen *child support* genannt. Der Begriff *best interest and welfare of the child* ist die Formel, nach der nahezu alle rechtlichen Entscheidungen beurteilt werden, an der Kinder beteiligt sind.

Im Englischen haben internationale Verträge (wie auch im Deutschen) viele
Synonyme:
- international agreements
- international treaties
- international conventions

d) Lernkontrolle

Bitte ergänzen Sie die englischen Begriffe:

Adoption

ähnlich

Anerkennung

anfechtbar

Annullierung

auf Grund von

Auflösung

Beendigung der Ehe

begrenzt

Behörde

daher

Ehe

Ehebruch

Ehefrau

Ehegatte

ehelicher Güterstand

Ehemann

elterliche Verantwortung

Entführung

Federführung, Schirmherrschaft

geregelt sein durch

in Betracht ziehen

internationale Konvention

internationales Übereinkommen

Kindeswohl

Kindesunterhalt   _____

Lebensunterhalt   _____

Maßnahme   _____

Minderjährige(r)   _____

nichtig, ungültig   _____

Scheidung   _____

Sorgerecht   _____

Sorgerecht zusprechen   _____

umfassen   _____

unbegrenzt   _____

Unterhalt   _____

Unterhalt(szahlungen) für den
Ehegatten   _____

Unterhaltsverpflichtung   _____

unüberbrückbar   _____

verlassen, im Stich lassen   _____

Vollstreckung   _____

Zuständigkeit   _____

Lösung siehe S. 136

H. Civil Procedure

I. In the Court Room

a) Text

The parties of the dispute, plaintiff and defendant, enter the court room together with their attorneys. Neither the jury, nor the judge is present, yet. The bailiff appears: "Please, rise!" The judge and the jury enter the court room. In his complaint the plaintiff claims 30 million US$ of punitive damages. He alleges that the drugs produced by the defendant's company have caused him physical harm. In his answer, the defendant denies every allegation the plaintiff has made. The jurors look at the plaintiff. He looks really miserable. The taking of evidence begins. The cause of action is negligence. The burden of proof is with the plaintiff. After the last plaintiff's witness has been questioned, the defendant's attorney calls a medical expert. He wants him to confirm that the drug in question could not have caused the harm alleged. Before the actual questioning of the expert, the plaintiff has the option to voir dire the expert. He has the right to do so because the expert has been appointed by the defendant. At the end of the trial the spokesman of the jury reads the verdict. Due to the preponderance of evidence they hold that the defendant is liable for the damage put forward by the plaintiff and also for pain and suffering. The amount for compensation, held by the jury, is 30 million US$. In his judgment the judge cuts the sum to 5 million US$.

b) Vokabeln zum Text

allegation	Behauptung
allege, to	behaupten
answer	Klageerwiderung
appoint, to	ernennen
attorney	Anwalt, Anwältin
bailiff	Gerichtsdiener/in
be liable for, to	haftbar sein für
be questioned, to	befragt werden
burden of proof	Beweislast
call, to	aufrufen
cause of action	*siehe unten*
cause, to	verursachen
claim, to	fordern
company	Unternehmen, Gesellschaft
compensation	Entschädigung

complaint	Klageschrift
confirm, to	bestätigen
court room	Gerichtssaal
damage	Schaden
damages for pain and suffering	Schmerzensgeld
defendant	Beklagte(r)
deny, to	bestreiten
dispute	Rechtsstreit
harm	Schaden
hold, to	befinden
in question	fraglicher/e/es
judgment	Urteil
medical expert	medizinische(r) Sachverständige(r)
negligence	*siehe unten*
party	Prozesspartei
physical harm	körperliche Schäden
plaintiff	Kläger/in
produce, to	produzieren
punitive damages	Strafschadensersatz
put forward, to	vorlegen
questioning	Befragung
spokesman	Sprecher
taking of evidence	Beweisaufnahme
the preponderance of evidence	überwiegende Beweise
trial	Gerichtsverhandlung
verdict	Juryentscheidung
voir dire	*siehe unten*
witness	Zeuge, Zeugin

c) Erläuterung der Fachterminologie

Die englische *cause of action* kommt der deutschen Anspruchsgrundlage nahe. Da allerdings das *common law*, anders als das *civil law*, eher prozessual denkt als materiell-rechtlich, sind die beiden Systeme im Hinblick auf die Begriffe Anspruchsgrundlage und *cause of action* nicht zu vergleichen. Es ist daher ratsam, entweder *cause of action* unübersetzt zu lassen oder einen neutralen deutschen Begriff wie z.B. „materiell-rechtliche Grundlage" zu verwenden.

Negligence sollte hier unbedingt unübersetzt bleiben, da dies der englische Begriff für eine *cause of action* ist, die weit mehr voraussetzt als nur die Fahrlässigkeit des Schädigers. Eine Übersetzung mit der nahliegenden „Fahrlässigkeit" wäre daher schlicht falsch. Das *voir dire* ist ebenfalls ein Rechtsinstitut, das das deutsche Recht nicht kennt. Es muss mangels sinnvoller Übersetzungsalternative unübersetzt bleiben. Das *voir dire* ist wieder auf dem *adversarial system* begründet. Dadurch, dass jede Partei ihren Sachverständigen berufen kann, hat die andere Partei das Recht, den Sachverständigen auf seine Expertise hin zu befragen, bevor er Angaben zum Verfahren macht. Darüber hinaus ist die andere Seite berechtigt, den Sachverständigen der Gegenseite auch zur Sache zu befragen.

Wie bereits in der Einheit zum Strafrecht erläutert, ist *the preponderance of evidence* der Maßstab, nach dem einer Zivilklage stattgegeben wird. Im Strafrecht liegt der Maßstab höher, nämlich bei *beyond a reasonable doubt*. Befragung kann im Englischen entweder *questioning* oder *interrogation* sein. Letztere wird eher im Strafrecht als Vernehmung oder Verhör verwendet. Die Zeugenaussage nennt man *deposition*.

d) Lernkontrolle

Bitte ergänzen Sie die englischen Begriffe:

Anwalt, Anwältin   _____

befragt werden   _____

Befragung (2×)   a) _____ b) _____

behaupten   _____

Behauptung   _____

Beklagte(r)   _____

bestätigen   _____

bestreiten   _____

Beweisaufnahme   _____

Beweislast   _____

einen Zeugen aufrufen   _____

Entschädigung   _____

Schadensersatz fordern   _____

fraglicher/e/es   _____

Gerichtsdiener/in   _____

Gerichtssaal   _____

Gerichtsverhandlung   _____

haftbar sein für   _____

Juryentscheidung   _____

Klageerwiderung   _____

Kläger/in   _____

Klageschrift   _____

körperliche Schäden   _____

medizinische(r) Sachverständige(r) _____

Prozesspartei   _____

Rechtsstreit   _____

Schaden (2×)   a) _____ b) _____

Schmerzensgeld   _____

Strafschadensersatz   _____

überwiegende Beweise   _____

Unternehmen, Gesellschaft   _____

Urteil   _____

verursachen   _____

vorlegen   _____

Zeuge, Zeugin   _____

Zeugenaussage   _____

Lösung siehe S. 138

II. From Complaint to Enforcement

a) Text

1. Pleadings: A civil action always starts with the plaintiff setting up a complaint. It contains at least one cause of action and provides an explanation of the plaintiff's demands from the defendant. In the US, it is the plaintiff's duty to serve the defendant with the complaint and the summons. The defendant then writes an answer, responding to the allegations in the complaint.

2. Pre-trial Discovery: The pre-trial discovery phase is entirely different from the German civil procedure process. The plaintiff must prove the facts necessary to establish the cause of action plead in the complaint. The defendant must prove the facts necessary to establish the defenses set forth in the answer. In pre-trial discovery, both parties must disclose the evidence they intend to use in the trial to prove the facts favorable to them, without being requested by the other party. In addition, the parties may request from the other party any evidence they determine to be relevant to the case, with some limitations. In the US, the details of pretrial discovery are governed by Rule 26 of the Federal Rules of Civil Procedure.

3. The Trial: After the pre-trial discovery, the jury is selected. It consists of 12 jurors. The 7th Amendment of the U.S. Constitution sets down a constitutional right to a jury trial. Each party has the right to challenge candidates who will then not become members of the jury. It is the jury's duty to evaluate the facts. After the parties' opening statements, the taking of evidence begins. Witnesses and expert witnesses are heard, documents are presented and the parties have the right to make their remarks. At the end of the trial the jury retreats for deliberations. After their verdict, the judge renders the judgment. In 95% of all cases, however, the dispute ends with a settlement.

4. Enforcement of the Judgment: Pursuant to the full faith and credit clause in the U.S. Constitution, a judgment rendered in one state can be enforced in any other state in the US if it is valid, final, and on the merits. Enforcing a US judgment in Germany, however, is a little more complicated. It has to be recognized according to § 328 German Code of Civil Procedure (ZPO) and enforced in compliance with §§ 722, 723 ZPO.

b) Vokabeln zum Text

according to	gemäß
allegation	Behauptung
answer	Klageerwiderung
cause of action	*siehe oben unter H.I.*
challenge, to	eine Einrede erheben gegen
civil action	Zivilklage, Zivilsache

complaint	Klageschrift
deliberation	Beratung
disclose, to	offenlegen
enforce, to	vollstrecken
evaluate, to	bewerten
final	endgültig
German Code of Civil Procedure	ZPO
in compliance with	in Übereinstimmung mit
limitation	Einschränkung
on the merits	zur Sache
pleadings	Schriftsätze
prove, to	beweisen
present, to	vorlegen
pursuant to	gemäß
recognize, to	anerkennen
remark	Anmerkung
render, to	erlassen
request, to	anfragen, anfordern, verlangen
retreat, to	sich zurückziehen
select, to	auswählen
serve, to	zustellen
set up, to	aufsetzen, verfassen
settlement	Vergleich
summons	Ladung
taking of evidence	Beweisaufnahme
valid	rechtskräftig

c) Erläuterung der Fachterminologie

Pursuant to ist ein weiteres Synonym für *according to* („gemäß"). Weitere wichtige zivilprozessuale Begriffe sind: *lis pendens* (Rechtshängigkeit) und *res judicata* (Rechtskraft).

d) Lernkontrolle

Bitte ergänzen Sie die englischen Begriffe:

anerkennen   _____

anfragen, anfordern, verlangen _____

Anmerkung   _____

aufsetzen, verfassen   _____

auswählen   _____

Behauptung   _____

Beweisaufnahme   _____

Beweise offenlegen   _____

beweisen   _____

bewerten   _____

die Klageerwiderung zustellen   _____

Dokumente vorlegen   _____

ein Urteil erlassen   _____

ein Urteil vollstrecken   _____

eine Einrede erheben gegen   _____

Einschränkung   _____

endgültig   _____

gemäß (2×)   a) _____ b) _____

in Übereinstimmung mit   _____

Klageerwiderung   _____

Klageschrift   _____

Ladung   _____

Rechtshängigkeit   _____

Rechtskraft   _____

rechtskräftig   _____

Schriftsätze   _____

sich zu Beratungen zurückziehen   _____

Vergleich   _____

Zivilklage, Zivilsache   _____

Zivilprozessordnung   _____

zur Sache   _____

Lösung siehe S. 139

I. Office Language

a) Text

I. In the Office

Corin: Good morning, Tracy.

Tracy: Morning, Corin. Have you seen the note Mr. Smith from the legal department left on my desk for me the other day?

Corin: No, I'm sorry. Your desk is such a mess. I'm surprised you still have room to fit your computer on it.

Tracy: Yes, me too. As a matter of fact, I'm having trouble finding all the office supplies I need. Yesterday I was looking for my hole punch and stapler, but all I found was some old paperclips and a broken ruler! Maybe I should run to the store and just buy it all new.

Corin: That sounds good. If you don't mind, could you get me some ring binders and folders? I also ran out of envelopes and highlighters. Oh, and a new eraser would be great.

Tracy: That's no problem.

Corin: Thanks. And in the meantime I will send you an e-mail and attach that file you asked me for yesterday.

Tracy: That'd be great, thank you. Could you also get a copy of that memo Hank circulated this morning? I didn't get one for some reason.
… Ok, I'll be back in a minute.

Corin: Ok, see you then.

II. On the Phone

Secretary: Rick Right's office, Susan Smith speaking. What can I do for you?

Mr. Wrong: This is Wilbert Wrong. Could you put me through to Mr. Right please? I'm afraid I'll need some legal assistance.

Secretary: If you hold the line just a moment, please, and I'll see if he's in.
…
I'm sorry, Mr. Right is not available at the moment. He's in a meeting and in the middle of negotiations. If you like, I could pass you on to Mrs. Good. She's Mr. Right's assistant.

Mr. Wrong: Thank you, but I need to speak to Mr. Right in person. When would it be a good time for me to call again?

Secretary: I suggest you try again this afternoon. We don't need to make an appointment. I'll give you his extension.

Mr. Wrong: Ok, thank you. I appreciate your help.

Secretary: You're welcome.

b) Vokabeln zum Text

appointment	Termin, Verabredung
appreciate, to	dankbar sein, schätzen
attach, to	anhängen
available	erreichbar
circulate, to	herumreichen, in Umlauf geben
desk	Schreibtisch
envelope	Umschlag
eraser	Radiergummi
extension	Durchwahl
file	Datei, Akte
folder	Schnellhefter
highlighter	Textmarker
hold the line, to	am Apparat bleiben
hole punch	Locher
in person	persönlich
legal assistance	Rechtsberatung, juristischer Rat
legal department	Rechtsabteilung
meeting	Besprechung, Sitzung
memo	Aktennotiz, -vermerk
negotiation	Verhandlung
note	Nachricht
office supply	Bürobedarf, -gegenstände
paperclip	Büroklammer
pass s.o. on to s.b., to	jmd. weiterleiten an
put s.o. through to s.b., to	jmd. durchstellen
ring binder	Ordner
ruler	Lineal
speaking	*hier:* am Apparat
stapler	Tacker
suggest, to	vorschlagen

c) Lernkontrolle

Bitte ergänzen Sie die englischen Begriffe:

Aktennotiz, -vermerk   _____

am Apparat bleiben   _____

anhängen   _____

Besprechung, Sitzung   _____

Briefumschlag   _____

Bürogegenstände, -bedarf   _____

Büroklammer _____

dankbar sein, schätzen _____

Datei, Akte _____

Durchwahl _____

erreichbar _____

Schnellhefter _____

in Umlauf geben, herumreichen _____

jmd. durchstellen _____

jmd. weiterleiten an _____

Lineal _____

Locher _____

Nachricht _____

Ordner _____

Radiergummi _____

Rechtsabteilung _____

Rechtsberatung, juristischer Rat _____

Schreibtisch _____

Tacker _____

Termin, Verabredung _____

Textmarker _____

Verhandlung _____

vorschlagen _____

Lösung siehe S. 141

Abschnittstest Nr. 3

Für die Bearbeitung der folgenden Aufgaben haben Sie 30 Minuten Zeit.

1 **Please fill in the gaps using the words from the list below**

> *alimony – annulment – child support – custody – division of property –*
> *divorce – encompasses – granted – irreconcilable – legal dissolution – void*

In the US, family law is governed by the states, rather than the federal government. Family law in most jurisdictions _____ , at a
minimum, the law of marriage, termination of marriage, _____
_____ , financial support, custody of children and adoption. Marriages can be terminated either by an _____
or a _____ . An annulment means that the marriage was
_____ or voidable from the start and, therefore, it is treated
as though it never existed. A divorce, on the other hand, is a _____
_____ of the relationship of husband and wife. In
most states, a divorce will be _____ on the basis of
adultery, desertion or cruel treatment, among other things. A "no-fault" divorce will be granted if the parties agree to terminate the marriage due to
_____ differences. In some cases, the court will
award _____ to one spouse – the money paid for
the maintenance of a spouse, for a definite or indefinite period of time. Similarly, if the couple has children, the court may decide to award custody and
_____ to one of the parties. In determining the
_____ of the children, the court must decide what is in
"the best interest and welfare" of the children.

2 **Please add the English equivalents**

Anerkennung   _____

anhängen   _____

begrenzt   _____

Behörde   _____

Beratung   _____

Besitzer/in   _____

bewegliche Sachen   _____

Beweisaufnahme   _____

Bürobedarf   _____

Ehebruch   _____

Ehegatte   _____

Ehemann   _____

Eigentum erwerben   _____

Eigentumsübergang   _____

endgültig   _____

Entführung   _____

erreichbar   _____

Forderung   _____

Grundstück   _____

in Übereinstimmung mit   _____

Juryentscheidung   _____

Kindesunterhalt   _____

Kläger/in   _____

Klageschrift   _____

Kreditsicherungsrecht   _____

nichtig, ungültig   _____

Prozesspartei   _____

Schaden   _____

Schnellhefter   _____

Schriftsätze   _____

Strafschadensersatz   _____

Tacker   _____

Termin   _____

umfassen   _____

unüberbrückbar   _____

Urteil   _____

Vergleich   _____

Verpflichtung   _____

vollstrecken   _____

zusprechen   _____

3 **Please explain in what way other areas of law are connected to property law**

_____

_____

_____

_____

_____

_____

_____

_____

_____

_____

_____

_____

_____

_____

_____

_____

_____

4 **Please translate into English**

Die Parteien des Rechtsstreits, Kläger und Beklagter, betreten mit ihren Anwälten den Sitzungsraum. Weder die Juroren noch der Richter sind bereits anwesend. Der Gerichtsdiener erscheint: *„Bitte erheben Sie sich!"* Der Richter und die Juroren betreten den Sitzungsraum. Der Kläger fordert in seiner Klageschrift 30 Millionen US$ Strafschadensersatz. Er behauptet, durch ein Medikament gesundheitliche Schäden erlitten zu haben, das im Unternehmen des Beklagten hergestellt worden war. Der Beklagte bestreitet in seiner Klageerwiderung alle Behauptungen des Klägers. Die Juroren betrachten den Kläger. Er sieht wirklich elend aus. Die Beweisaufnahme beginnt. Die Anspruchsgrundlage ist „*negligence*". Die Beweislast liegt beim Kläger. Nachdem der letzte Zeuge des Klägers befragt worden ist, ruft der Beklagtenvertreter einen medizinischen Sachverständigen auf. Er soll bestätigen, dass das Medikament die behaupteten Schäden nicht ausgelöst haben kann. Am Ende der Verhandlung verliest der Sprecher der Jury ihren Spruch. Aufgrund der überwiegenden Beweise befinden sie, dass der Beklagte dem Kläger für den von ihm vorgebrachten Schaden und für die erlittenen Schmerzen haftet. Die von der Jury zugesprochene Entschädigungssumme ist US$ 30 Mio. Der Richter senkt die Summe in seinem Urteil auf US$ 5 Mio.

Lösung siehe S.154

J. Abschlussklausur

Für die Bearbeitung der folgenden Aufgaben haben Sie 120 Minuten Zeit.

1 Please fill in the gaps using the words in the list below

> *apartment – assignee – assignment – assignor – borrower – contract of employment – employer – goods – interest – lease – lender – money – purchase price – rent – salary – sales contract – seller – services – tenant*

contract	parties		objects	
sales contract				
loan				
lease				
assignment (not a contract)				–
contract of employment				

2 Please fill in the gaps using the words below

> *balances – branch – consisted – declared – defense – Executive – former – held – interests – justice – led – power – protect – pursuing – representing – separated*

On July 4, 1776, following the American Revolution, the _____

colonies in the New World cut ties with England and _____ their

independence. The "Constitutional Convention" that ultimately produced

today's U.S. Constitution was _____ in Philadelphia in 1787.

The Convention _____ of 55 delegates, _____

a wide variety of _____ and backgrounds. George Washing-

ton _____ the Convention, whose members were determined to

_____ liberty, establish _____ and provide for

their common _____. In _____ these objectives,

the delegates agreed that the government's _____ should be

_____ into three branches: Legislature, _____,

and Judiciary. A system of checks and _____ was created to prevent any single _____ from becoming too powerful.

3 | Bitte notieren Sie mit Hilfe der englischen Erklärungen die englischen Begriffe der gesuchten Rechtsgebiete.

Beispiel: Money collected by the government from the people without giving something in return is called taxes. There is an almost unlimited list of taxes, such as income tax, sales tax, value added tax, inheritance tax.

Area of law: **tax law** _____

1. This aspect of law provides rules for the formation and performance or non-performance of agreements between private persons.

   Area of law: _____

2. History repeats itself. This is one reason why it is important to know about the past, especially as a lawyer.

   Area of law: _____

3. Two big companies agree on a price for a product they both sell on the market. By doing so they don't have to fear competition and consumers are forced to pay a higher price.

   Area of law: _____

4. Here you find rules for the jurisdiction of a court to hear a certain case, to render a judgment and how to enforce a civil judgment.

   Area of law: _____

5. Obligations between states can arise when they conclude international contracts with each other. Also human rights belong to the field of ...

   Area of law: _____

6. The probably most popular area of law: it defines what is considered a crime, and how different crimes are to be punished.

   Area of law: _____

7. When a person dies, his or her property is transferred to his wife or her husband and to his or her children.

   Area of law: _____

8. The main source of law in this area is the supreme law of every country.

   Area of law: _____

9. We need this area in order to prevent our soil, plants, animals, and natural resources from being exploited, polluted and eventually destroyed.

    Area of law: _____

10. A certain legal aspect might be dealt with differently in Germany, France, or the US.

    Area of law: _____

11. This is the law governing divorce or child support.

    Area of law: _____

12. When an accident occurs and the victim claims money from the other side, we are legally in the area of ...

    Area of law: _____

13. When someone works for somebody else, both the rights and responsibilities are governed by...

    Area of law: _____

14. Whenever two parties from different countries enter into a relationship governed by private law, the law that is applicable to the legal problems must first be determined.

    Area of law: _____

15. This area of law governs questions such as whether a person has ownership or possession of a thing.

    Area of law: _____

4 **Reading comprehension: Please read Exkurs 2 on page 112/113 twice and answer the following questions in full sentences. What are the differences, what are the similarities of ius commune and common law?**

_____

_____

_____

_____

_____

_____

_____

_____

_____

_____

_____

_____

5 **Please translate into English**

Der Gerichtsdiener führt den Angeklagten auf seinen Platz. Er ist des Mordes ersten Grades angeklagt. Die 12 Juroren beobachten jede Bewegung. Der Bezirksstaatsanwalt erhebt sich. Er hat vor zwei Monaten gegen den Beklagten Anklage erhoben. Er beginnt damit, dem Angeklagten und der *Jury* die Anklageschrift vorzulesen. Nach dem Eröffnungsplädoyer des Bezirksstaatsanwalts hält der Verteidiger seinen Eröffnungsvortrag. Jede Seite ist fest entschlossen, den Fall für sich zu gewinnen. Die Verteidigung ruft ihren ersten Zeugen auf. Langsam geht der Zeuge zum Zeugenstand. Nun hat der Staatsanwalt die Gelegenheit zum Kreuzverhör. Doch darauf hat der Verteidiger den Zeugen schon vorbereitet. Sie haben tagelang mögliche Fragen des Staatsanwalts besprochen. Nichts sollte dem Zufall überlassen bleiben. Am Ende des Prozesses erklärt der Richter der *Jury* die Rechtslage, und die Juroren ziehen sich zu ihren Beratungen zurück. Nun ist es an ihnen zu entscheiden, ob die vorgebrachten Tatsachen und die Beweise genügen, um den Angeklagten schuldig zu sprechen. Ihnen ist klar, im Zweifel gilt die Vermutung, dass der Angeklagte unschuldig ist. Nur wenn sie alle ohne jeden vernünftigen Zweifel davon ausgehen, dass er das Verbrechen begangen hat, lautet ihr Urteilsspruch „schuldig".

_____

_____

_____

_____

_____

_____

_____

_____

_____

_____

_____

_____

_____

_____

_____

_____

_____

_____

6 **Please add the respective English and German terms to the following amendments**

Amendment I: Congress shall make no law respecting an establishment of religion, or prohibiting the free exercise thereof; or abridging the freedom of speech, or of the press; or the right of the people peaceably to assemble, and to petition the Government for a redress of grievances.

freedom of speech – freedom of the press – ~~prohibition of the establishment of religion~~ – right to free exercise of religion – right to peaceably assemble – right to petition

Meinungsfreiheit – Petitionsrecht – Pressefreiheit – Religionsausübungsfreiheit – ~~Verbot der Gründung einer Staatsreligion~~ – Versammlungsfreiheit

English	German equivalent
prohibition of the establishment of religion	Verbot der Gründung einer Staatsreligion

Amendment VI: In all criminal prosecutions, the accused shall enjoy the right to a speedy and public trial, by an impartial jury of the State and district wherein the crime shall have been committed, which district shall have been previously ascertained by law, [...] and to have the Assistance of Counsel for his defence.

district of court shall be previously ascertained – right to a public trial – right to a speedy trial – right to an impartial jury – right to counsel for his defense

Beschleunigungsgrundsatz – existiert so nicht – Öffentlichkeitsgrundsatz – Recht auf Pflichtverteidiger – Teil des Grundsatzes des gesetzlichen Richters

English	German equivalent

7 **Please fill in the gaps using the words in the list below**

> *actually – called – chattel – contracts – distinguish – divided – equals – immovable property – inheritance – intangible – lead – linked – movable property – patents – personal property – principle of separation and abstraction – property – real estate – tangible – things – unlike*

Property law is closely _____ to many other areas of law such as the law of _____, the law of secured transactions, or the law of _____, the latter also _____ law of succession. This link is even closer in common law legal systems than in German law because, _____ in German law, in most common law legal systems there is no _____

_____, which would separate and _____ between two different kinds of contracts: those that _____ to an obligation to transfer _____, and those that _____ transfer the property. The law of property is also relevant for bankruptcy law.

_____ are _____ into separate categories: There is _____ and _____.

Movable property includes for example cars, clothes, chairs and tables, immovable property is pieces of land, also called _____.

Both movable and immovable property have synonyms: movable property equals _____, immovable property _____ real property. Movable property might be _____ or _____. Tangible movable property is called _____. Examples for intangibles are _____.

8 **Please add the English equivalent**

Abtretung _____

Allgemeine Geschäfts-
bedingungen _____

anfechtbar _____

Angebot _____

Anzahlung _____

Arbeitnehmer/in _____

ausdrücklich _____

ausreichend, hinreichend _____

bedeutend _____

bei Erhalt der Ware _____

Beklagte(r) _____

Besitz aufgeben _____

Besitzstörung _____

Betrug _____

Beweis _____

Bundesrecht _____

darlegen, vorschreiben _____

Darlehen _____

Darlehensnehmer/in _____

ehelicher Güterstand _____

Einbruchdiebstahl _____

einen Vertrag schließen _____

einschränken _____

Einwilligung _____

Ergebnis _____

erwerben, erhalten _____

etwas in Betracht ziehen _____

Federführung, Schirmherrschaft _____

gegen jmd. Anklage
erheben _____

Geldstrafe _____

Gerichtsdiener/in   _____

gewährleisten, bereitstellen,
beinhalten   _____

Gewährleistung(srecht)   _____

Grundstück   _____

haftbar gemacht werden für   _____

Irrtum   _____

jmd. in Untersuchungshaft
nehmen   _____

jmd. ins Kreuzverhör nehmen   _____

Kanzlei   _____

Kindeswohl   _____

Klageerwiderung   _____

Klageschrift   _____

Laien   _____

Nothilfe   _____

Querschnitt   _____

rechtsprechende Gewalt   _____

Rechtsquelle   _____

Rechtsstreit   _____

rechtsverbindlich   _____

Richter/in   _____

Scheidung   _____

Scheitern, Ausbleiben   _____

Schmerzensgeld   _____

Sicherungsrecht   _____

Sorgerecht   _____

Strafverfahren   _____

Strafverteidiger/in   _____

überzeugend   _____

ungeachtet   _____

ungerechtfertigte Bereicherung   _____

Unterhalt   _____

Unterhaltsverpflichtung   _____

verhandeln _____

verklagt werden wegen _____

Verlassen, Imstichlassen _____

verletzen _____

Verordnung _____

Versuch _____

Verwaltungsrecht _____

Vollstreckung _____

vorbringen _____

vorsätzlich, absichtlich _____

Waren _____

Wille, Absicht _____

Zeuge, Zeugin _____

Zivilklage, Zivilsache _____

zur Sache _____

zusprechen _____

9 | Please translate into German

Family law in most jurisdictions encompasses, at a minimum, the law of marriage, termination of marriage, matrimonial property, financial support, custody of children and adoption. Marriages can be terminated either by an annulment or a divorce. An annulment means that the marriage was void or voidable from the start and, therefore, it is treated as though it never existed. A divorce, on the other hand, is a legal dissolution of the relationship of husband and wife. In most states, a divorce will be granted on the basis of adultery, desertion or cruel treatment, among other things. A "no-fault" divorce will be granted if the parties agree to terminate the marriage due to irreconcilable differences. In some cases, the court will award alimony to one spouse – the money paid for the maintenance of a spouse, for a definite or indefinite period of time. Similarly, if the couple has children, the court may decide to award custody and child support to one of the parties. In determining the custody of the children, the court must decide what is in "the best interest and welfare" of the children.

_____

_____

_____

_____

_____

_____

_____

_____

_____

_____

_____

_____

_____

_____

_____

_____

_____

_____

_____

_____

_____

10 **Please fill in the gaps using the words from the list below**

> *arrested – arson – attempt – burglary – consented – custody – defense –*
> *fraud – intimidation – misdemeanours – mistake – motives – murder –*
> *offenses – robbery – self-defense – shoplifting – source – suspects – takes –*
> *theft – trial – victim*

The area of criminal law is what every non-lawyer seems to be most interested in. It provides a _____ for many novels and movies. Which one of the _____ committed the crime? What were his _____? Who was the _____? Minor crimes are called _____, minor offenses are called _____. Most of the time the suspect is _____ after he has accomplished the crime. But even the _____ to commit a crime can be punished. In certain cases the suspect can be taken into _____ and put into jail until the end of his _____, especially in serious and intentional crimes such as _____, rape or _____. A murder can be first-degree when it is committed in a particularly malicious way. Minor offenses are e.g. assault and battery, _____, defamation or _____.

A theft that is committed in a supermarket is called _____

and if a thief breaks into someone else's house in order to steal things it is

called a _____. If violence or _____ is used against

a person while the offender _____ away the person's property it

is called _____. In his _____ the suspect might allege

that he acted in _____ or defense of another, or that the

victim _____ to his conduct. Further, he may have acted in

this certain way by _____.

11 **Please translate into German**

*Most of the time the suspect is arrested after he has accomplished the crime.
But already the attempt of a crime can be punished. In certain cases the suspect can be taken into custody and put into jail until the end of his trial, especially for serious and intentional crimes like murder, rape or arson.*

_____

_____

_____

_____

_____

Lösungen siehe S. 158

Exkurs 1
Das Übersetzen juristischer Texte

Das Übersetzen juristischer Texte ist anspruchsvoller als zunächst vielleicht vermutet. Juristische Begriffe (*terms*) sind immer eng mit den dahinterstehenden Konzepten (*notions*) verbunden. Haben die juristischen Konzepte (*notions*) des einen Rechtssystems einen anderen Inhalt als im anderen, wird aber in der Übersetzung ohne ergänzende Erklärung der entsprechende linguistische Begriff (*term*) verwendet, so kann der im ausländischen Recht unerfahrene Leser Gefahr laufen, die juristische Bedeutung des Begriffs falsch zu verstehen. Dieses Risiko besteht nicht nur bei so genannten *false friends*. Das Übersetzen juristischer Texte kommt also nicht ohne hinreichende rechtsvergleichende Kenntnisse aus. Daher sollte man folgende Regeln bei jeder Übersetzung im Hinterkopf behalten:

1. Nicht-juristische Begriffe: Nicht-juristische Begriffe müssen zwar auch sorgfältig übersetzt werden, das Risiko der Sinnverfälschung eines juristischen Textes ist hier aber eher gering.

2. Juristische Begriffe, bei denen die zugrunde liegenden juristischen Konzepte in den beiden betreffenden Rechtssystemen zumindest vergleichbar sind: Diese Wörter können übersetzt werden. Ihnen sollten aber u.U. ergänzende Erklärungen in Klammern folgen.

Beispiel: Ein Beispiel für diese Kategorie ist der deutsche Begriff „Vertrag", der wegen der Vergleichbarkeit der juristischen Konzepte dahinter ohne Gefahr mit *contract* übersetzt werden kann.

3. Juristische Begriffe, die in den beiden betreffenden Rechtssystemen unterschiedliche Bedeutungen haben: Wörter dieser Kategorie dürfen auf keinen Fall übersetzt werden! Dem unübersetzt belassenen englischen Begriff kann ggf. in Klammern eine Warnung folgen, dass er nicht mit dem deutschen juristischen Begriff XY gleichgesetzt werden darf.

Beispiel: Der Begriff *consideration* kommt dem deutschen Begriff der „Gegenleistung" zwar oberflächlich betrachtet nahe. Nach genauerer Recherche verschwindet aber unsere Gegenleistung hinter dem ausgreifenden und in seiner Bedeutung für den gesamten Vertrag des anglo-amerikanischen Rechts entscheidenden Konzept der *consideration*. Die beiden Begriffe sind also in ihrer Bedeutung innerhalb der jeweiligen Rechtssysteme nicht vergleichbar. Eine Übersetzung muss daher unterbleiben.

4. Juristische Begriffe des einen Rechtssystems, die im anderen Rechtssystem unbekannt sind: Bei juristischen Begriffen, die im jeweils anderen Rechtssystem unbekannt sind, besteht nur ein geringes Risiko, juristisch falsch zu übersetzen. Falls die Sprache des Rechtssystems, das das betreffende juristische Konzept nicht kennt, einen passenden Begriff enthält, kann dieser verwendet werden, muss aber nicht. Falls nicht, bleibt er auf jeden Fall unübersetzt.

Beispiel: Als Beispiel seien hier die *punitive damages* des US-amerikanischen Rechts angeführt. Dies ist eine Form des Schadensersatzes, durch die der Beklagte für sein besonders verwerfliches Verhalten bestraft werden soll. Diese Vorstellung ist dem deutschen Schadensersatzrecht weitgehend fremd. Es gibt hier traditioneller Weise keinen Schadensersatz mit strafender Funktion. Eine Verwechslungsgefahr besteht daher nicht. So bleibt es dem Übersetzenden frei, die *punitive damages* unübersetzt zu übernehmen oder das deutsche (ungefährliche) Wort „Strafschadensersatz" zu verwenden.

Exkurs 2
Ius Civile/Ius Commune = Civil Law/Common Law?

Civil law und *common law* sind aus verschiedenen Rechtstraditionen hervorgegangen. Die rechtsgeschichtlichen Begriffe *ius civile* und *ius commune* und deren linguistische Ähnlichkeit mit den Rechtskreisen *civil law* und *common law* erfordern eine genauere Auseinandersetzung mit den jeweils dahinterstehenden Konzepten, um eine Vermengung oder gar eine Gleichsetzung der vermeintlichen Begriffspaare zu verhindern.

Vom *ius civile* zum *ius commune* als Basis für das *civil law*

Civil law hat seine Basis im römischen Recht. Hier wurde das *ius civile* (Bürgerrecht – Recht der römischen Bürger) vom *ius gentium* (Recht anderer Volkszugehöriger) getrennt. Je nach Zugehörigkeit der betroffenen Person wurde das eine oder das andere angewandt. Der römische Kaiser Justinian ließ die Regeln des *ius civile* im *Codex Iuris Civilis* zusammenfassen.

Dieses Sammelwerk wurde im Hochmittelalter „wiederentdeckt". In der ersten europäischen Universität in Bologna (gegründet 1185) wurden Rechtswissenschaftler im *ius civile* ausgebildet; bald strömten Interessierte aus ganz Europa nach Bologna und studierten und diskutierten das Recht und bildeten es weiter, sodass es bald die Eigenständigkeit erlangte, die es bis heute hat. Äußerst begünstigend war dabei der Umstand, dass zur damaligen Zeit Latein die in ganz Europa einheitlich gängige Wissenschaftssprache war.

Bei ihrer Rückkehr in ihre Heimatländer brachten die nun Rechtsgelehrten die Rechtsvorstellungen aus Bologna mit und verbreiteten sie an ihren Heimatuniversitäten (z. B. Würzburg, gegründet 1402). Es entstand im Laufe der Jahrhunderte ein einheitliches europäisches Rechtssystem, das *ius commune*, wegen der Art und Weise seiner Entstehung auch **gelehrtes Recht** genannt.

Das *ius commune* fand Eingang in die deutsche Reichskammergerichtsordnung von 1495, die festlegte, dass das *ius commune* anzuwenden ist, wenn das primär anzuwendende Partikularrecht nicht festgestellt werden kann.

Das *common law*

Zeitlich vor dem kontinental-europäischen *ius commune* entwickelte sich in England ein anderes Rechtssystem, das *common law*. Der normannische König Henry II (zweite Hälfte des 12. Jh.) führte umfangreiche Modernisierungen des Staats- und Verwaltungswesens ein, zu denen auch das *common law* gehörte. In England war formalisiertes Recht (*law*) grundsätzlich eine Angelegenheit des Königs; Lücken wurden durch *equity* geschlossen. Das *common law* ist praxisbasiert und anwendungsbezogen (bis heute starke Bedeutung der Präzedenzfälle). Im Gegensatz zur kontinentalen Verwissenschaftlichung wurde in England das Recht als Handwerk und die juristische Ausbildung als *apprenticeship* gesehen.

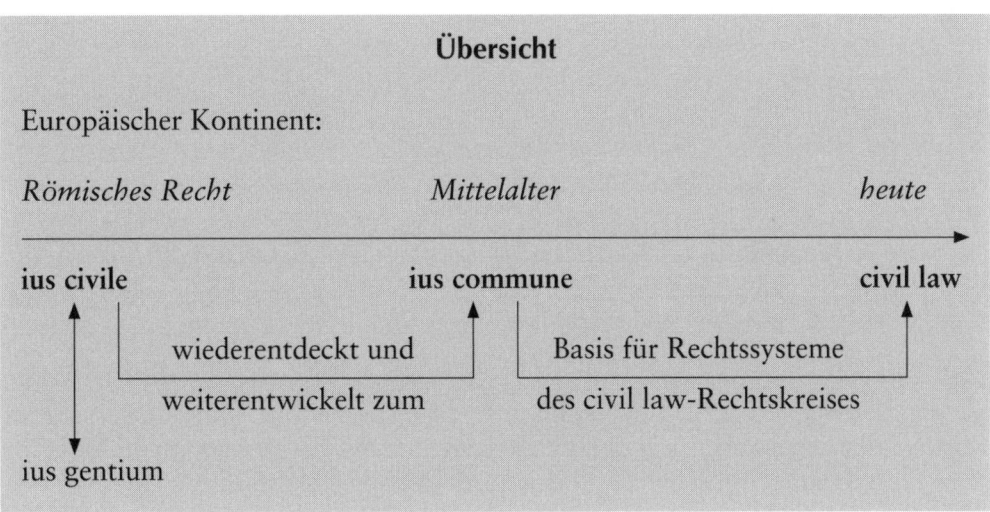

K. Lösungsvorschläge

A. General Legal Terms (S. 1)

I. Common Law and Civil Law (S. 4)

annehmen, übernehmen, rezipieren	to adopt
beeinflussen	to influence
Begriff (2×)	a) term b) notion
begründet sein auf, basieren	to be based on
bindende gerichtliche Entscheidung	binding court decision
erachten, ansehen als, berücksichtigen	to consider
Fallrecht, Rechtsprechung	case law
Gericht	court
Gerichtsentscheidung	court decision
Gesetz (3×)	a) law b) statute c) act
hybrides/gemischtes Rechtssystem	hybrid legal system
infolgedessen, im Ergebnis	as a result
jedoch	however
Präzedenzfall	precedent
Rahmen	framework
Recht	law
Rechtskreis	legal tradition
Rechtsquelle	source of law
Rechtssystem	legal system
Richterrecht	judge-made law
sich beziehen auf	to refer to
sich unterscheiden	to differ
überwiegend	predominantly
unabhängig	independent
unterscheiden, differenzieren	to draw a distinction
während, wohingegen	whereas

Übung Areas of Law (S. 5)

1. administrative law	Verwaltungsrecht
2. antitrust	Kartellrecht
3. civil procedure	Zivilprozessrecht
4. commercial law	Wirtschaftsrecht
5. company law	Gesellschaftsrecht
6. comparative law	Rechtsvergleichung
7. conflict of laws	Internationales Privatrecht
8. constitutional law	Verfassungsrecht
9. contracts	Vertragsrecht
10. copyright law	Urheberrecht
11. criminal law	Strafrecht
12. criminal procedure	Strafprozessrecht
13. criminology	Kriminologie
14. E.C. law	Europ. Gemeinschaftsrecht
15. employment law	(Individual-)Arbeitsrecht
16. environmental law	Umweltrecht
17. family law	Familienrecht
18. intellectual property	Gewerblicher Rechtsschutz
19. labo(u)r law	Kollektives Arbeitsrecht
20. law of obligations	Schuldrecht
21. law of succession	Erbrecht
22. legal history	Rechtsgeschichte
23. legal philosophy	Rechtsphilosophie
24. patent law	Patentrecht
25. property	Sachenrecht
26. public international law	Völkerrecht
27. tax law	Steuerrecht
28. torts	Deliktsrecht
29. unfair competition	Unlauterer Wettbewerb
30. unjust enrichment	Ungerechtf. Bereicherung

II. Lernkontrolle Vokabeln (S. 7)

aufgrund, wegen	due to
Deliktsrecht	a) torts b) delict
Entsprechung, Pendant	equivalent
Erbrecht (2×)	a) inheritance law b) law of succession
Europäisches Gemeinschaftsrecht	European Community law (E. C. law)
Gesellschaftsrecht	company law
(Individual-)Arbeitsrecht	employment law
Internationales Privatrecht (2×)	a) conflict of laws b) private international law
Kartellrecht	antitrust
Kollektives Arbeitsrecht	labo(u)r law
Öffentliches Recht	public law
Patentrecht	patent law
Privatrecht	private law
Rechtsgeschichte	legal history
Rechtsvergleichung	comparative law
Sachenrecht	property
Schuldrecht	law of obligations
Steuerrecht	tax law
Strafprozessrecht	criminal procedure
Strafrecht	criminal law
Umweltrecht	environmental law
Ungerechtfertigte Bereicherung	unjust enrichment
Unlauterer Wettbewerb	unfair competition
Urheberrecht	copyright law
Verfassungsrecht	constitutional law
Verwaltungsrecht	administrative law
Völkerrecht	public international law
Wirtschaftsrecht	commercial law
Zivilprozessrecht	civil procedure

III. Development of US Law (S. 11)

Akt der Gesetzgebung	legislative act
anwenden	to apply
ausführende Gewalt	executive power
Beziehung	relation
daher (2×)	a) therefore b) thus
das Recht, Waffen zu tragen	the right to bear arms
ein Gesetz erlassen (2×)	a) to pass a law b) to enact
ein Recht ausüben	to exercise a right
Einwanderer, Einwanderin	immigrant
erachten	to consider
erklären, eine E. abgeben	to declare
erlauben	to permit
Freiheit (2×)	a) freedom b) liberty
jedoch	however
Gesetz (3×)	a) law b) statute c) act
gesetzgebendes Organ	legislative body
gesetzgebende Gewalt	legislature/legislative power
gewährleisten, bereitstellen	to provide for
Grundrecht	fundamental right/basic right
in Kraft treten (2×)	a) to enter into effect b) to come into force
Inkrafttreten	entry into force
Praktiker/in	practitioner
rechtsprechende Gewalt	judiciary/judicial power
Redefreiheit	freedom of speech
regeln	to govern
Regelung, Norm, Bestimmung	provision
Religionsfreiheit	freedom of religion
Streitigkeit (2×)	a) controversy b) dispute
Trennung von Kirche und Staat	separation of church and state
Unabhängigkeitserklärung	Declaration of Independence
unterzeichnen	to sign
Ursprung, Wurzel	root
Verfassung	constitution

Verfassungszusatz	amendment
verfolgen	to persecute/to pursue/to prosecute
wählen (2×)	a) to elect b) to vote
Wissenschaftler/in, Gelehrte(r)	scholar

IV. Sources of Law (S.16)

Abkürzung	abbreviation
Anwalt, Anwältin	lawyer
abweichen von	to deviate from
Auslegung (2×)	a) interpretation b) construction
Befugnisse auf jmd. übertragen	to confer power on s.o.
Begründung	reasoning
d.h.	i.e.
demzufolge, im Ergebnis	as a result
ein Urteil erlassen	to render a judgment
eine Ansicht zum Ausdruck bringen	to express a view
Entscheidung	decision
Entwurf	draft
etw. in einem Rechtswörterbuch nachschlagen	to look sth. up in a legal dictionary
Fallrecht, Rechtsprechung	case law
ff.	et seq.
geregelt sein durch	to be governed by
Gerichtsbezirk i.w.S.	jurisdiction
Gesetzentwurf	bill
Gesetzgebungsgewalt	legislative power
Gewohnheitsrecht	customary law
in Betracht ziehen	to take into consideration
Insolvenzrecht	bankruptcy law
jemandem vorbehalten sein	to be reserved to s.o.
juristische Zeitschrift (2×)	a) law review b) law journal
juristischer Aufsatz	legal article
Juryentscheidung	verdict
Kartellrecht	antitrust

Lehrbuch (2×)	a) treatise b) hornbook
primäre Rechtsquelle	primary source of law
Rechtsgebiet	area of law
Rechtssystem	legal system
Regierung	government
Schrifttum, Literatur	doctrine
Streitigkeit (2×)	a) dispute b) controversy
u. a.	et al.
überwiegend	predominantly
überzeugend	persuasive
Urteil	judgment
Verordnung	regulation
verpflichtet sein, etwas zu tun	to be obliged to do sth.
Verpflichtung	obligation
z. B.	e. g.
zu einem gewissen Grad	to a certain degree

V. Legal Education and Legal Professions (S. 20)

Angeschuldigte(r)	accused
ausstellen	to issue
Beendigung	completion
berechnen, in Rechnung stellen	to charge
Eigentumsübertragung	transfer of title
eine Streitigkeit entsteht	a dispute arises
einen Mandanten vor Gericht vertreten	to represent a client before court
Ergebnis	outcome
ernennen	to appoint
ersterer/e/es	former
Gebühr	fee
gegen jemanden Anklage erheben	to bring charges against s.o.
Gesellschaft, Unternehmen	company
Jura studieren	to study law
Jurist/in, Anwalt, Anwältin	lawyer
Kanzlei	law firm

Mandant/in	client
Notar/in	notary
Praktikum	a) internship b) legal training
Rechtsanwalt, Rechtsanwältin (5×)	a) attorney b) solicitor c) barrister d) counsel e) advocate
Schadensersatz	damages
Staatsanwalt, Staatsanwältin	public prosecutor
Strafverfahren	criminal proceedings
verhandeln	to negotiate
wählen	to elect

B. Constitutional Law (S. 23)

I. The U.S. Constitution (S. 24)

bestehen aus	to constist of
Delegierte(r), Abgeordnete(r)	delegate
eine Versammlung abhalten	to hold a convention
entschlossen sein	to be determined
erklären	to declare
Freiheit	a) freedom b) liberty
gemäß	according to
Gerechtigkeit	justice
Gewaltenteilung	separation of powers
gründen, schaffen	to establish
Kanzler/in	chancellor
letztendlich, schließlich	ultimately
Macht, Befugnis	power
Macht übertragen an	to vest power in
Mitglied	member
Regierung	government
schützen	to protect
trennen	to separate
Unabhängigkeit	independence
Verbindungen abbrechen zu	to cut ties with
verfolgen	to pursue
verhindern	to prevent
Verteidigung	defense
vertreten	to represent
Ziel (2×)	a) objective b) goal

II. The Bill of Rights (S. 28)

ansteigen, sich erhöhen	to increase
aufgrund	due to
bedeutend	significant
Befugnisse	powers
bewahren	to preserve
beziehungsweise	respectively
ein Gesetz billigen	to approve a law
Bürger/in	citizen
Bürgerrechte	civil rights
darf nicht (2×)	a) shall not b) may not
delegieren, übertragen	to delegate
einen Anspruch haben auf	to be entitled to
einschränken	to abridge
Forderung	demand
freie Ausübung	free exercise
Freiheit	freedom/liberty
friedlich	peaceably
ein Recht garantieren	to guarantee a right
gerecht	just
Gesetzesänderung	amendment
Grundrecht (2×)	a) basic right b) fundamental right
im Folgenden	in the following
in Beziehung auf, im Hinblick auf	respecting
kann	may
Menschenrechte	human rights
muss	shall
Pressefreiheit	freedom of the press
Redefreiheit	freedom of speech
regeln	to regulate
Regelung, Bestimmung	provision
Religionsfreiheit	freedom of religion
schützen	to protect
sichern, absichern, sicherstellen	to ensure
Strafverfahren	criminal proceedings

verändern	to alter
verbieten	to prohibit
Verfassungszusatz	amendment
verletzen (3×)	a) to breach b) to infringe c) to violate
versammeln	to assemble
verweigern	to refuse
Volk	people
vorbehalten sein	to be reserved

III. Further Amendments (S. 32)

anerkennen (2×)	a) to acknowledge b) to recognize
abschaffen	to abolish
anwendbar sein auf	to apply to
Bevölkerung	population
Bürgerkrieg	civil war
demzufolge	as a result
Der Staatsvertrag wurde ratifiziert.	the international treaty was ratified
Die Sklaverei wurde abgeschafft.	slavery was abolished
die Verfassung sieht vor, dass …	the Constitution provides that
ein neues Gesetz einführen	to introduce a new law
ein Recht verletzen	to violate/infringe a right
ein Recht zusprechen	to grant a right
einschränken	to abridge
einzelner	individual
etwas unterliegen	to be subject to sth.
halten für, vermuten (3×)	a) to deem b) to assume c) to presume
Gleichbehandlungsgrundsatz	equal-protection-clause
im Vergleich zu	in comparison to
im Verlauf	over the course of
Jahrhundert	century
jedoch	however
rechtmäßig verurteilt (*strafrechtlich*)	duly convicted
Rechtsstaatsprinzip	rule of law

Schutz	protection
sich konzentrieren auf	to focus on
ungeachtet des Geschlechts	regardless of sex
verweigern, vorenthalten	to deny
zusätzlich, darüber hinaus	in addition

C. Criminal Law and Criminal Procedure (S. 43)

I. Crime, Offense and Misdemeanour (S. 45)

anzünden, brandstiften	to set on fire
Attentat	assassination
Attentäter/in	assassin
begehen	to commit
Beleidigung	defamation
Betrug	fraud
betrügen (2×)	a) to deceive b) to defraud
böswillig, heimtückisch	malicious
Brandstiftung	arson
Dieb/in	thief
Diebstahl	theft
einbrechen	a) to burgle b) to break in
Einbrecher/in	burglar
Einbruchdiebstahl	burglary
Einwilligung	consent
Gefängnis	jail
Gerichtsverhandlung	trial
Gewalt	violence
Haftbefehl	arrest warrant
handeln	to act
Irrtum	mistake
jemanden in Untersuchungshaft nehmen	to take someone into custody
jemanden verhaften/festnehmen	to arrest someone
Körperverletzung (2×)	a) assault b) battery
Ladendiebstahl	shoplifting
minderes Vergehen, Ordnungs-widrigkeit	misdemeano(u)r
Mord mit bedingtem Vorsatz	second-degree murder

Mord (2×)	a) murder b) homicide
Mörder/in	murderer
Nichtjurist/in	non-lawyer
Nothilfe	defense of another
Notwehr	self-defense
Opfer	victim
Raub	robbery
schwer (2×)	a) first-degree b) aggravated
stehlen	to steal
Strafgefangene(r)	convict
Straftat, Delikt, Verbrechen	crime
Täter/in	offender
Tatverdächtige(r)	suspect
Totschlag	manslaughter
Unterlassen	omission
Vergehen, Delikt	offense
Vergewaltigung	rape
Verhalten	conduct
Versuch	attempt
vollendet	accomplished
vorsätzlich, absichtlich	intentional
zu seiner Verteidigung	in his defense

II. Who Are All These People in the Court Room? (S. 49)

Argument	argument
aufteilen	to divide
hinreichende Beweise	sufficient evidence
Behauptung	allegation
Bezirksstaatsanwalt	district attorney (DA)
das beste Ergebnis erzielen	to achieve the best outcome
Daten, Angaben	data
eine(n) Sachverständige(n) benennen	to appoint an expert witness
Entscheidungsbefugnis	decision-making power
Ergebnis (2×)	a) outcome b) result

(erwiesene) Tatsache	fact
Fachleute	professionals
Geschworenenverhandlung	jury trial
günstig	favourable
in dem Bestreben, etw. zu tun	in an effort to do sth.
Jurist/in	lawyer
Laien	lay people
Querschnitt der Gesellschaft	cross section of society
repräsentieren, vertreten	to represent
Richter/in	judge
Staatsanwalt, -anwältin	prosecutor
stattdessen	instead
Strafvertreidiger/in	defense attorney
um zu	in order to
Verhandlung	trial
vor Gericht erscheinen	to appear before court
vorbringen	to put forth
Zeuge, Zeugin	witness
zusammengesetzt sein aus	to be composed of

III. A Day in Court (S. 52)

Angeklagte(r) (2×)	a) defendant b) accused
Anklage erheben gegen	to bring charges against
Anklageschrift	indictment
Anklagepunkt, Anschuldigung	accusation
etwas auferlegen	to impose something
einen Zeugen aufrufen	to call a witness
jemanden für schuldig befinden	to find someone guilty
einen Zeugen befragen	to examine a witness
Beratung	deliberation
Eröffnungsplädoyer vortragen	to present an opening statement
etwas besprechen, immer wieder durchgehen	to review something
beziehungsweise	respectively

Bezirk	district
den Zeugenstand betreten	to take the stand
ein Recht genießen	to enjoy the right
ein Verbrechen begehen	to commit a crime
erwerben, erhalten	to obtain
wegen etwas angeklagt sein	to be charged with
fordern, erfordern	to require
gegenübergestellt werden	to be confronted with
Geldstrafe	fine
Gerichtsdiener/in	bailiff
Geschworene(r)	juror
im Vorhinein gesetzlich bestimmt	previously ascertained by law
jmd. für schuldig befinden	to find someone guilty
jmd. ins Kreuzverhör nehmen	to cross-examine s. o.
Kaution, Sicherheitsleistung	bail
mit Bezug zu	with reference to
Mord	murder
Schuldspruch der Jury	verdict
sich erheben	to rise
sich zurückziehen	to retreat
Strafe verhängen	to inflict punishment
Strafverfolgung, Strafverfahren	criminal prosecution
Strafverteidiger/in	defense attorney
über jeden vernünftigen Zweifel hinaus	beyond a reasonable doubt
überzeugen	to convince
unparteiisch	impartial
unverhältnismäßig hoch	excessive
Verbrechen	crime
Verteidigung	defence
zu seinen Gunsten	in his favour
zügige und öffentliche Verhandlung	speedy and public trial
zwingend	compulsory

D. Contracts, Sales Law and Secured Transactions (S. 55)

I. Contracts (S. 58)

Abtretung	assignment
Angebot	offer
Annahme	acceptance
Arbeitgeber/in	employer
Arbeitnehmer/in	employee
Arbeitsvertrag	employment contract
ausdrücklich	express
benötigen, erfordern	require, to
daher, deshalb	thus
Darlehen	loan
Darlehensgeber/in	lender
Darlehensnehmer/in	borrower
der Vertrag ist anfechtbar	the contract is voidable
einbringen, beitragen	supply, to
einen Vertrag schließen (3×)	a) to enter into a contract b) to conclude a contract c) to make a contract
Einigung, Vereinbarung	agreement
Einwendung	defense
Erfüllung	specific performance
erstgenannter/e/es	former
Fall, Umstand	instance
Falschbehauptung	misrepresentation
Forderung	receivable
Gehalt	salary
Geschäft	transaction
Gläubiger/in	creditor
Grundstückskaufvertrag	contract for the sale of land
im Gegensatz zu	unlike

Irrtum	mistake
jmd. etwas übertragen	confer s.th. on s.o., to
Kauf	purchase
Käufer/in	buyer
Kaufpreis	purchase price
Kaufvertrag	sales contract
konkludent, stillschweigend	implied
letztgenannter/e/es	latter
Lohn	wages
Miete	rent
Mieter/in	tenant
Mietvertrag	lease
mündlich	orally
Nichterfüllung	non-performance
nichtig	void
Nutzen	benefit
Rechtsgrundlage	legal basis
Rückzahlung	back-payment
Schadensersatz	damages
Schenkung	gift
schriftlich	in writing
Schuldner/in	debtor
sich einigen über	agree on, to
sowohl ... als auch	both ... and
Täuschung	fraud
Umstände des Falls	circumstances of the case
Verkauf	sale
Verkäufer/in	seller
Vermieter/in	landlord/landlady
vermuten	to assume
Versprechen	promise
Vertrag	contract
Vertragspartei	party
Waren	goods
Wert	value
Wille, Absicht	intent

Zedent/in	assignor
Zessionar/in	assignee
Zinsen	interest
zugrunde liegen	underlie, to
zusätzlich	in addition

II. Buying and Selling (S. 63)

Allgemeine Geschäftsbedingungen (2×)	a) standard terms b) general terms and conditions
Anzahlung	down payment
bei Erhalt der Ware	on receipt of the goods
Einzelhändler/in	retailer
Ersatzteil	spare part
etwas auf Kredit kaufen	to buy something on credit
fehlerhaft, mangelhaft	defective
Geschäftspartner/in	business partner
Gewährleistung(srecht)	warranty
Gewinn	profit
Großhändler/in	wholesaler
Hersteller/in (2×)	a) manufacturer b) producer
kaufen (2×)	a) to buy b) to purchase
Kaufpreis	purchase price
Kreditsicherungsrecht	law of secured transactions
Kunde, Kundin	customer
liefern	to deliver
maximieren	maximize, to
Rate	instalment
schicken, versenden	to ship
schriftlich	in writing
sicherstellen	ensure, to
Sicherungsgut	collateral
Sicherungsrecht	security interest
Sicherungsvertrag	security agreement
Verbraucher/in	consumer

Vertragsverletzung	breach of contract
was … betrifft	as to …
Zustand der Waren	condition of the goods

E. Torts and Damages (S. 67)

Abschreckung	deterrence
arglistig, betrügerisch	fraudulent
begehen, verüben	commit, to
Beklagte(r)	defendant
Besitzstörung	trespass
böswillig, heimtückisch	malicious
Einwendung, Einrede	defense
Einwilligung	consent
fahrlässig	negligent
Fahrlässigkeit	negligence
fehlerhaftes Produkt	defective product
Gefährdungshaftung	strict liability
geschehen, sich ereignen	occur, to
haftbar gemacht werden	be held liable, to
Klage aus unerlaubter Handlung	tort action
Kläger/in	plaintiff
kompensatorischer Schadensersatz	compensatory damages
Mitverschulden	contributory negligence
Notwehr	self-defense
rechtliche Grundlage	legal basis
Schädiger/in	tortfeasor
Schmerzensgeld	damages for pain and suffering
Strafe, Bestrafung	punishment
Strafschadensersatz	punitive damages
Unrecht	wrong
Unternehmen, Gesellschaft	company
verklagt werden wegen	be sued for, to
Verletzung (2×)	a) harm b) injury
Verleumdung	slander
Verschulden	fault
Vorsatz, Absicht	intention
vorsätzlich	intentional

F. Property (S. 77)

Besitz	possession
Besitz aufgeben (2×)	a) relinquish possession b) surrender possession
Besitz ergreifen	take possession
Besitz erlangen	gain possession
Besitz wiederaufnehmen	resume possession
Besitzentziehung	dispossession
Besitzer/in	possessor
Besitzstörung	trespass
bewegliche Sachen	a) movable property b) personal property
Eigent. an e. Grundstück übertragen	to convey
Eigentum (3×)	a) property b) ownership c) title
Eigentum erwerben	to acquire
Eigentümer/in (2×)	a) owner b) proprietor
Eigentumsübergang	passing of title
Eigentumsübertragung (2×)	a) transfer of title b) transfer of property
Eigentumsvermutung	presumption of title
Eigentumsvorbehalt (2×)	a) retention of title b) reservation of title
Forderung	receivable
Grundstück (2×)	a) piece of land b) real estate
gutgläubiger Erwerb	bona fide purchase
in Besitz bleiben	remain in possession
körperliche Gegenstände (2×)	a) tangible property b) chattels
Nachlass	estate
Sache	thing
stören, beeinträchtigen	to interfere with
Trennungs- und Abstraktionsprinzip	principle of separation and abstraction
trotzdem, nichtsdestotrotz	nevertheless
unbewegliche Sachen	a) immovable property b) real property
unkörperliche Gegenstände	intangible property
Vermögen (3×)	a) assets b) estate c) property

G. Family Law (S. 81)

Adoption	adoption
ähnlich	similarly
Anerkennung	recognition
anfechtbar	voidable
Annullierung	annulment
auf Grund von	due to
Auflösung	dissolution
Beendigung der Ehe	termination of marriage
begrenzt	definite
Behörde	authority
daher	therefore
Ehe	marriage
Ehebruch	adultery
Ehefrau	wife
Ehegatte	spouse
ehelicher Güterstand	matrimonial property
Ehemann	husband
elterliche Verantwortung	parental responsibility
Entführung	abduction
Federführung, Schirmherrschaft	auspice
geregelt sein durch	to be governed by
in Betracht ziehen	to take into consideration
internationale Konvention	international convention
internationales Übereinkommen	international agreement
Kindeswohl	the best interest and welfare of the child
Kindesunterhalt	child support
Lebensunterhalt	maintenance
Maßnahme	measure
Minderjährige(r)	minor
nichtig, ungültig	void

Scheidung	divorce
Sorgerecht	custody
Sorgerecht zusprechen	to award custody
umfassen	to encompass
unbegrenzt	indefinite
Unterhalt	financial support
Unterhalt(szahlungen) für den Ehegatten	alimony
Unterhaltsverpflichtung	maintenance obligation
unüberbrückbar	irreconcilable
verlassen, im Stich lassen	desertion
Vollstreckung	enforcement
Zuständigkeit	jurisdiction

H. Civil Procedure (S. 83)

I. In the Court Room (S. 85)

Anwalt, Anwältin	attorney
befragt werden	to be questioned
Befragung (2×)	a) questioning b) interrogation
behaupten	to allege
Behauptung	allegation
Beklagte(r)	defendant
bestätigen	to confirm
bestreiten	to deny
Beweisaufnahme	taking of evidence
Beweislast	burden of proof
einen Zeugen aufrufen	to call a witness
Entschädigung	compensation
Schadensersatz fordern	to claim damages
fraglicher/e/es	in question
Gerichtsdiener/in	bailiff
Gerichtssaal	court room
Gerichtsverhandlung	trial
haftbar sein für	to be liable for
Juryentscheidung	verdict
Klageerwiderung	answer
Kläger/in	plaintiff
Klageschrift	complaint
körperliche Schäden	physical harm
medizinische(r) Sachverständige(r)	medical expert
Prozesspartei	party
Rechtsstreit	dispute
Schaden (2×)	a) harm b) damage
Schmerzensgeld	damages for pain and suffering

Strafschadensersatz	punitive damages
überwiegende Beweise	the preponderance of evidence
Unternehmen, Gesellschaft	company
Urteil	judgment
verursachen	to cause
vorlegen	to put forward
Zeuge, Zeugin	witness
Zeugenaussage	deposition

II. From Complaint to Enforcement (S. 88)

anerkennen	to recognize
anfragen, anfordern, verlangen	to request
Anmerkung	remark
aufsetzen, verfassen	to set up
auswählen	to select
Behauptung	allegation
Beweisaufnahme	taking of evidence
Beweise offenlegen	to disclose evidence
beweisen	to prove
bewerten	to evaluate
Dokumente vorlegen	to present documents
eine Einrede erheben gegen	to challenge
Einschränkung	limitation
endgültig	final
gemäß (2×)	a) pursuant to b) according to
in Übereinstimmung mit	in compliance with
Klageerwiderung	answer
die Klageerwiderung zustellen	to serve the answer
Klageschrift	complaint
Ladung	summons
Rechtshängigkeit	lis pendens
Rechtskraft	res judicata
rechtskräftig	valid
Schriftsätze	pleadings

sich zu Beratungen zurückziehen	to retreat for deliberations
Vergleich	settlement
ein Urteil erlassen	to render a judgment
Zivilklage, Zivilsache	civil action
Zivilprozessordnung	Code of Civil Procedure
zur Sache	on the merits

I. Office Language (S. 92)

Aktennotiz, -vermerk	memo
am Apparat bleiben	to hold the line
anhängen	to attach
Besprechung, Sitzung	meeting
Briefumschlag	envelope
Bürogegenstände, -bedarf	office supply
Büroklammer	paper clip
dankbar sein, schätzen	to appreciate
Datei, Akte	file
Durchwahl	extension
erreichbar	available
Schnellhefter	folder
in Umlauf geben, herumreichen	to circulate
jmd. durchstellen	to put someone through to someone
jmd. weiterleiten an	to pass someone on to someone
Lineal	ruler
Locher	hole punch
Nachricht	message, note
Ordner	ring, binder
Radiergummi	eraser
Rechtsabteilung	legal department
Rechtsberatung, juristischer Rat	legal assistance
Schreibtisch	desk
Tacker	stapler
Termin, Verabredung	appointment
Textmarker	highlighter
Verhandlung	negotiation
vorschlagen	to suggest

K. Lösungsvorschläge Abschnittstests

Abschnittstest Nr. 1 (S. 34)

1 Please fill in the gaps using the words below

> *applied – binding – case law – common law – customary law – government – holding – judgment – obligation – parliament – persuasive authority – primary – reasoning – regulations – rendered – stare decisis – statutes*

Sources of _____**common law**_____ legal systems are the same as those in any civil law legal system. There is positive law which is either passed by ___**parliament**___ – so called ___**statutes**___, or by the ___**govern-ment**___ – so called ___**regulations**___. Beside positive law there is also ___**case law**___ which, based on the principle of ___**stare decisis**___, is ___**binding**___ to lower courts of the same jurisdiction. Case law ___**rendered**___ by courts of another jurisdiction is considered to be ___**persuasive authority**___. Following this concept there is no ___**obligation**___ for the court of jurisdiction A to follow the ___**holding**___ and the ___**reasoning**___ of a ___**judgment**___ rendered by a court in jurisdiction B. In addition to positive law and case law as ___**primary**___ sources of law there is, to a minor degree, also ___**customary law**___ which can be ___**applied**___ to a dispute.

2 Please translate into English

Der Kongress darf kein Gesetz verabschieden, das die Gründung von Religionsgemeinschaften zum Gegenstand hat oder die freie Religionsausübung verbietet; oder die Meinungs-, oder Pressefreiheit; oder das Recht der Menschen, sich friedlich zu versammeln, einschränkt.

Congress shall make no law respecting an establishment of religion, or prohibiting the free exercise thereof; or abridging the freedom of speech, or of the press; or the right of the people peaceably to assemble.

3 **Please add the English equivalent**

abschaffen	to abolish
abweichen	to deviate from
Angeschuldigte(r)	accused
anwenden	to apply
Auslegung	interpretation, construction
Befugnisse/Macht übertragen	to vest powers
Begründung	reasoning
das Recht, Waffen zu tragen	the right to bear arms
Deliktsrecht	torts, delict
Eigentumsübertragung	transfer of title
ein Gesetz erlassen, verabschieden	to pass an act, a law, a statute
eine Entscheidung erlassen	to render a decision
einen Anspruch haben auf	to be entitled to
einschränken	to abridge
entstehen, aufkommen	to arise
Entwurf	draft
Forderung	demand
Gebühr	fee
gemäß	according to
Gesetz (3×)	a) law b) statute c) act
Gesetzentwurf	bill
Gewerblicher Rechtsschutz	intellectual property
Gewohnheitsrecht	customary law
Grundrechte	basic rights, fundamental rights
im Vergleich zu	in comparison to
im Verlauf von	over the course of
Internationales Privatrecht	conflict of laws, private international law
Kartellrecht	antitrust
Mandant/in	client
rechtmäßig verurteilt (strafrechtlich)	duly convicted
Rechtsvergleichung	comparative law
Regelung	provision
Schadensersatz	damages
stammen von, sich ableiten von	to derive from

überwiegend	predominantly
unlauterer Wettbewerb	unfair competition
unterscheiden	to draw a distinction
verfolgen	to pursue, to persecute, to prosecute
verhandeln	to negotiate
verweigern	to refuse, to deny
Völkerrecht	public international law
vorsehen, dass/regeln, dass	to provide that
Ziel	objective, goal

4 **Please explain the three meanings (notions) of the term „common law" (in full sentences)**

Für die Lösung siehe S. 3

5 **Please translate into German**

The United States, as it exists today, was founded in 1789, when its Constitution entered into effect. In 1620 the Pilgrims fled Europe because they had not been permitted to freely exercise their religion. As the US began to develop, it became clear that legislative acts, being passed by a legislative body that had not even been elected, would have taken much too long. Thus, it was preferable to apply English case law to US controversies than it was to apply no law during the years it would have taken to pass legislation. Therefore, even after declaring independence from England, the new states, with one exception (Louisiana), continued to apply English law. Louisiana, however, created a civil code modelled on the French *code civil*. To this day, Louisiana's legal system follows the civil law legal tradition.

Die Vereinigten Staaten in ihrer heutigen Gestalt wurden 1789 gegründet, als ihre Verfassung in Kraft trat. Im Jahre 1620 flüchteten die Pilgrims (Pilgerväter) aus Europa, da ihnen nicht erlaubt war, ihre Religion frei auszuüben. Als die Vereinigten Staaten sich zu entwickeln begannen, wurde klar, dass Legislativakte, verabschiedet von einem Gesetzgebungsorgan, das noch nicht einmal gewählt worden war, viel zu lange gedauert hätten. Somit war es vorzugswürdiger, englisches Fallrecht auf US-amerikanische Streitigkeiten anzuwenden, als gar kein Recht für die Jahre, die es für die Gesetzgebung gebraucht hätte. Deshalb wendeten die neuen Staaten, mit Ausnahme Louisianas, auch nach der Unabhängigkeitserklärung gegenüber England, weiterhin englisches Recht an. Louisiana jedoch schuf ein bürgerliches Gesetzbuch nach dem Vorbild des französischen Code civil. Bis zum heutigen Tag folgt Louisianas Rechtssystem der civil law-Tradition.

6 **Please fill in the four gaps underlined**

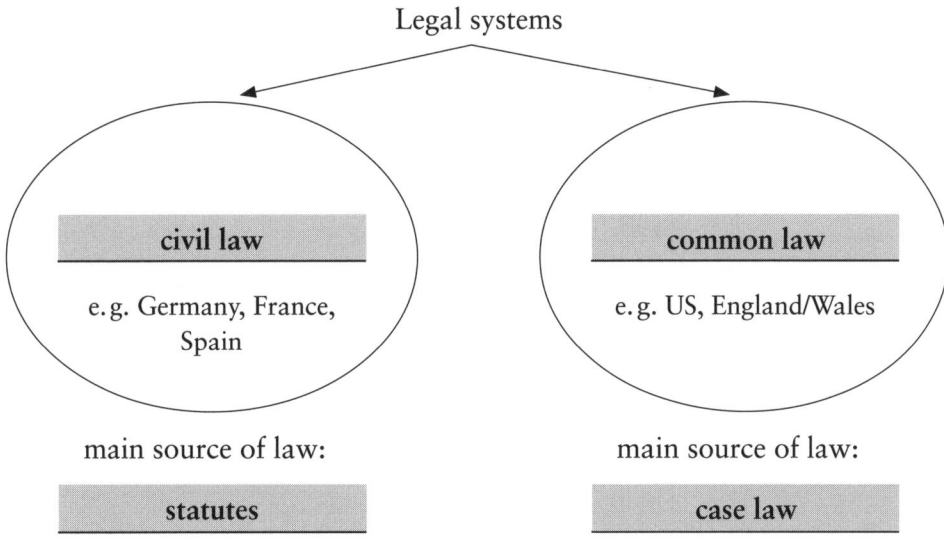

Legal systems

civil law

e.g. Germany, France, Spain

common law

e.g. US, England/Wales

main source of law:

statutes

main source of law:

case law

7 **Bitte ordnen Sie die Rechtsgebiete soweit möglich dem Privatrecht oder dem Öffentlichen Recht zu und ergänzen Sie die deutsche Übersetzung. Orientieren Sie sich bei der Einordnung an der universitären Fächereinteilung der Vorlesungen**

administrative law – antitrust – civil procedure – commercial law – company law – comparative law – conflict of laws – constitutional law – contracts – copyright law – criminal law – criminal procedure – criminology – E.C. law – employment law – environmental law – family law – intellectual property – labo(u)r law – law of obligations – law of succession – legal history – legal philosophy – patent law – property – public international law – tax law – torts – unfair competition – unjust enrichment

Arbeitsrecht – Deliktsrecht – Erbrecht – Europäisches Gemeinschaftsrecht – Familienrecht – Gesellschaftsrecht – Gewerblicher Rechtsschutz – Internationales Privatrecht – Kartellrecht – Kollektives Arbeitsrecht – Kriminologie – Patentrecht – Rechtsgeschichte – Rechtsphilosophie – Rechtsvergleichung – Sachenrecht – Schuldrecht – Steuerrecht – Strafprozessrecht – Strafrecht – Umweltrecht – Ungerechtfertigte Bereicherung – Unlauterer Wettbewerb – Urheberrecht – Verfassungsrecht – Vertragsrecht – Verwaltungsrecht – Völkerrecht – Wirtschaftsrecht – Zivilprozessrecht

Private Law		Public Law	
antitrust	Kartellrecht	*administrative law*	Verwaltungsrecht
civil procedure	Zivilprozessrecht	*constitutional law*	Verfassungsrecht
commercial law	Wirtschaftsrecht	*criminal law*	Strafrecht
company law	Gesellschaftsrecht	*criminal procedure*	Strafprozessrecht
conflict of laws	Internationales Privatrecht	*criminology*	Kriminologie
contracts	Vertragsrecht	*E.C. law*	Europ. Gemeinschaftsrecht
copyright law	Urheberrecht	*environmental law*	Umweltrecht
employment law	Arbeitsrecht	*public international law*	Völkerrecht
family law	Familienrecht	*tax law*	Steuerrecht
intellectual property	Gewerbl. Rechtsschutz	**Neutral**	
labo(u)r law	Kollektives Arbeitsrecht	*comparative law*	Rechtsvergleichung
law of obligations	Schuldrecht	*legal history*	Rechtsgeschichte
law of succession	Erbrecht	*legal philosophy*	Rechtsphilosophie
patent law	Patentrecht		
property	Sachenrecht		
torts	Deliktsrecht		
unfair competition	Unlauterer Wettbewerb		
unjust enrichment	Ungerechtf. Bereicherung		

8 | **Please translate into English**

Neben den primären Rechtsquellen gibt es auch sekundäre Rechtsquellen. Juristen sind nicht verpflichtet, den Ansichten zu folgen, die in sekundären Rechtsquellen zum Ausdruck kommen. Häufig jedoch sind sie bei der Suche nach einer Lösung zu einem rechtlichen Problem hilfreich. Dies ist der Grund, warum Juristen das so genannte Schrifttum, d.h. juristische Aufsätze und Ansichten, die Juraprofessoren in Lehrbüchern zum Ausdruck bringen, zu Rate ziehen. Kleinere Lehrbücher werden *hornbooks* genannt. Wenn jemand, der innerhalb des *common law*-Rechtskreises arbeitet, etwas über die Auslegung eines bestimmten rechtlichen Begriffs herausfinden muss, schaut er häufig in einem Wörterbuch oder spezieller in einem Rechtswörterbuch nach. Das berühmteste Rechtswörterbuch in den USA ist *Black's Law Dictionary*.

Besides the primary sources of law there are also secondary sources of law.

Lawyers are not obliged to follow views expressed in secondary sources.

Often, however, they are helpful to find a solution to a legal problem. This is

why lawyers consult the so called doctrine, i.e. law review articles and views

law school professors express in treatises. Smaller treatises are called

hornbooks. If someone practicing within the common law legal tradition has to find out about the interpretation of a certain legal term, he often

looks it up in a dictionary or more specifically in a legal dictionary. The

most famous legal dictionary in the US is "Black's Law Dictionary".

9 Reading Comprehension: Please read Exkurs 1 on page 110/111 twice and explain in your own words where to be careful when translating legal texts from one language to the other and when it is safe to do so. Please give examples

_____

_____

_____

_____

_____

_____

_____

_____

_____

_____

_____

_____

_____

10 Please fill in the gaps using the words below

appear – assistant – associate – barrister – charge – clerk – clients – company – contracts – conveyancers – country – court – damages – outcome – partner – solicitor

A lawyer can work e.g. as an _____**associate**_____ at a law firm, as in-house counsel within a _____**company**_____, as a _____**clerk**_____ at a court or as a notary. A clerk is an _____**assistant**_____ to a judge. In-house counsels negotiate _____**contracts**_____ for their company and represent it before _____**court**_____, if a legal dispute arises. Associate is the name for a lawyer working at a law firm before he eventually becomes a _____**partner**_____ in that firm. People working as a "Rechtsanwalt" are called differently, depending on the _____country_____ in which they work. It is _____solicitor_____ and _____barrister_____ in England, advocate in Scotland, attorney in the US, attorney and advocate in South Africa, depending on the court they can _____appear_____ before, and counsel and advocate in Namibia, again depending on the court they can appear before. Lawyers preparing the transfer of title for land are called _____conveyancers_____. From time to time some lawyers take on cases from _____clients_____ who are too poor to pay the lawyer's fee. This is called *"pro bono"*. Lawyers in the US _____charge_____ their clients on the basis of contingency fees. This means that their fee depends on the _____outcome_____ of the case. For example, if the client gets a high sum of _____damages_____, the lawyer will get between 30 and 50% of this sum. If the client loses the case, the lawyer will get nothing.

Fehler-Noten-Relation:

Fehler	Notenpunkte
0–1	18
2	17
3	16
4	15
5	14
6	13
7	12
8–9	11
10–11	10
12–13	9
14–15	8
16–17	7
18–19	6
20–22	5
23–25	4
26–35	3
36–45	2
46–50	1
>51	0

Mistakes: _____ Grade: _____

Abschnittstest Nr. 2 (S. 69)

1 Please translate into English

Verträge sind die Grundlage für viele Aspekte des Lebens. So einigen sich zum Beispiel Vermieter und Mieter darüber, dass der Mieter im Austausch gegen den monatlichen Mietzins im Haus des Vermieters wohnt, der Verkäufer und der Käufer einigen sich über den Kauf von Waren im Austausch gegen einen Kaufpreis, Arbeitgeber und Arbeitnehmer einigen sich darüber, dass der Letztere Dienstleistungen gegenüber dem Ersteren im Austausch gegen Gehalt erbringt, und der Darlehensgeber leiht dem Darlehensnehmer Geld im Austausch gegen zusätzlich zur Rückzahlung anfallende Zinsen. Die rechtliche Grundlage für diese Einigungen ist ein Vertrag: der Mietvertrag, der Kaufvertrag, der Arbeitsvertrag und der Darlehensvertrag. Ein Vertrag erfordert sowohl ein Angebot als auch eine Annahme.

Contracts underlie many aspects of life. For example, landlords and tenants agree on the tenant living in the landlord's house in exchange for a monthly rent, sellers agree with buyers on a sale of goods in exchange for a purchase price, employers and employees agree on the latter to perform services for the former in exchange for a salary and lenders lend money to borrowers in exchange for additional interest to the backpayment of the money. The legal basis of these agreements is a contract: the lease, the sales contract, the employment contract and the loan. A contract requires both an offer and an acceptance.

2 Please add the English equivalent

Angeklagte(r)	defendant
Anklage erheben gegen	to bring charges against
Anklageschrift	indictment
Annahme	acceptance
auferlegen	to impose
Behauptung	allegation
Beleidigung	defamation
Brandstiftung	arson
den Zeugenstand betreten	to take the stand
der Vertrag ist nichtig	the contract is void

Entscheidungsbefugnis	decision-making power
Eröffnungsplädoyer	opening statement
fehlerhaftes Produkt	defective product
Gerichtsverhandlung	trial
Gläubiger/in	creditor
Hersteller/in	manufacturer
jmd. verhaften	to arrest someone
jmd. etwas übertragen	to confer on
Kaufpreis	purchase price
Kaution, Sicherheitsleistung	bail
konkludent, stillschweigend	implied
Körperverletzung	assault
Kreditsicherungsrecht	law of secured transactions
Kunde, Kundin	customer
Ladendiebstahl	shoplifting
öffentliche Verhandlung	public trial
Recht auf Verhandlung vor einer jury	right to a jury trial
Sachverständige(r)	expert witness
Schenkung	gift
schwere Körperverletzung	aggravated assault
Strafgefangene(r)	convict
unparteiisch	impartial
Verhalten	conduct
Vermieter/in	landlord
Vertragserfüllung	specific performance
Vertragsverletzung	breach of contract
vollendet	accomplished
zwingend	compulsory

3 **Please add the respective counterpart**

offer	–	acceptance
tenant	–	landlord/landlady
express	–	implied
creditor	–	debtor
in writing	–	orally
assignor	–	assignee
borrower	–	lender
seller	–	buyer
employer	–	employee
goods	–	purchase price

4 **Please fill in the gaps using the words below**

achieve – allegations – appear – appointed – DA – decision – defense attorney – elected – evidence – expert witnesses – explain – judge (2×) – jury – lawyer – prosecutor – representing – trial

In the US, unlike in Germany, the _____ **judge** _____ plays a neutral role during a trial. Instead, it is the _____ **prosecutor** _____ (also called "the district attorney" or "_ **DA** _") and the _____ **defense attorney** _____ who put forth the _____ **evidence** _____ and the arguments in an effort to _____ **achieve** _____ the most favorable outcome for their position. In a jury _____ **trial** _____, the _____ **decision** _____-making power is divided between the judge and the jury. The jury is composed of 12 people _____ **representing** _____ a cross section of society. The _____ **jury** _____ decides which _____ **allegations** _____ are based on sufficient evidence to become fact, and they apply the law as it is explained to them by the _____ **judge** _____ to those facts. A judge in the US does not have to be a _____ **lawyer** _____. In many states, state court judges are _____ **elected** _____ by the people. Witnesses who _____ **appear** _____ before court in order to _____ **explain** _____ specific technical or medical data to the judge and the jury, are called _____ **expert witnesses** _____. Unlike the German system, expert witnesses in the US are not _____ **appointed** _____ by court, rather they are chosen by each party.

5 **Please add the respective English terminology**

	Delikt	Täter	Handlung
Brandstiftung	arson	arsonist	to set on fire
Attentat	assassination	assassin	to assassinate
Körperverletzung	assault	–	to assault
Einbruchdiebstahl	burglary	burglar	to burgle, to break in
Beleidigung	defamation	–	to insult s.o., to defame s.o.
Betrug	fraud	fraud, defrauder	to deceive, to defraud
Mord	murder	murderer	to murder, to kill
Vergewaltigung	rape	rapist	to rape someone
Raub	robbery	robber	to rob
Ladendiebstahl	shoplifting	shoplifter	to shoplift
Diebstahl	theft	thief	to steal

6 **Please translate into German**

A murder can be first-degree when it is committed in a particularly malicious way. Minor offenses are e.g. assault and battery, fraud, defamation or theft. If a theft is committed in a supermarket it is called shoplifting and if the thief broke into someone else's house in order to steal things it becomes a burglary and if he uses violence or intimidation against a person while he takes away the person's property it is called robbery. In his defense the suspect might allege that he has acted in self-defense or defense of another, or that the victim has consented to his conduct. Also he might have acted in this certain way by mistake.

Ein Mord kann ersten Grades sein, wenn er in einer besonders heimtückischen Art und Weise begangen wurde. Minder schwere Vergehen sind Körperverletzung, Betrug, Beleidigung und Diebstahl. Wenn ein Diebstahl z. B. in einem Supermarkt begangen wurde, wird er Ladendiebstahl genannt und wenn der Dieb in das Haus eines anderen eingebrochen ist, um Sachen zu stehlen, wird es Einbruchdiebstahl und wenn er Gewalt oder Drohung gegen eine Person anwendet, während er das Eigentum einer anderen Person wegnimmt, nennt man dies Raub. Zu seiner Verteidigung könnte der Tatverdächtige behaupten, dass er in Notwehr oder Nothilfe gehandelt hat oder dass das Opfer in sein Verhalten eingewilligt hat. Vielleicht hat er sich auch aufgrund eines Irrtums so verhalten.

7 **Please explain the term "cross-examination"**

Für die Lösung siehe bitte S. 52

Fehler-Noten-Relation:

Fehler	Notenpunkte
0–1	18
2	17
3	16
4	15
5	14
6	13
7	12
8–9	11
10–11	10
12–13	9
14–15	8
16–17	7
18–19	6
20–22	5
23–25	4
26–35	3
36–45	2
46–50	1
>51	0

Mistakes: _____   Grade: _____

1 Please fill in the gaps using the words from the list below:

*alimony – annulment – child support – custody – division of property –
divorce – encompasses – granted – irreconcilable – legal dissolution – void*

In the US, family law is governed by the states, rather than the federal government. Family law in most jurisdictions __encompasses__ , at a minimum, the law of marriage, termination of marriage, __division of property__ , financial support, custody of children and adoption. Marriages can be terminated either by an __annulment__ or a __divorce__ . An annulment means that the marriage was __void__ or voidable from the start and, therefore, it is treated as though it never existed. A divorce, on the other hand, is a __legal dissolution__ of the relationship of husband and wife. In most states, a divorce will be __granted__ on the basis of adultery, desertion or cruel treatment, among other things. A "no-fault" divorce will be granted if the parties agree to terminate the marriage due to __irreconcilable__ differences. In some cases, the court will award __alimony__ to one spouse – the money paid for the maintenance of a spouse, for a definite or indefinite period of time. Similarly, if the couple has children, the court may decide to award custody and __child support__ to one of the parties. In determining the __custody__ of the children, the court must decide what is in "the best interest and welfare" of the children.

2 Please add the English equivalents

Anerkennung	recognition
anhängen	to attach
begrenzt	definite
Behörde	authority

Beratung	deliberation
Besitzer/in	possessor
bewegliche Sachen	personal property
Beweisaufnahme	taking of evidence
Bürobedarf	office supply
Ehebruch	adultery
Ehegatte	spouse
Ehemann	husband
Eigentum erwerben	to acquire property
Eigentumsübergang	passing of title
endgültig	final
Entführung	abduction
erreichbar	available
Forderung	receivable
Grundstück	real estate
in Übereinstimmung mit	in compliance with
Juryentscheidung	verdict
Kindesunterhalt	child support
Kläger/in	plaintiff
Klageschrift	complaint
Kreditsicherungsrecht	law of secured transactions
nichtig, ungültig	void
Prozesspartei	party
Schaden	harm
Schnellhefter	folder
Schriftsätze	pleadings
Strafschadensersatz	punitive damages
Tacker	stapler
Termin	appointment
umfassen	to encompass
unüberbrückbar	irreconcilable
Urteil	judgment
Vergleich	settlement
Verpflichtung	obligation
vollstrecken	to enforce
zusprechen	to award

3 **Please explain in what way other areas of law are connected to property law**

Property is connected to the law of contracts. In common law legal

systems the ownership passes with the formation of the sales contract and

the delivery of the goods. However, according to German law a different

kind of contract is required because of the principle of separation and

abstraction. Property is also connected to bankruptcy law, since the power

to transfer title is taken away from the owner as soon as bankruptcy

proceedings are commenced. Also, property law is connected to family law,

in particular to matrimonial property, since there are different approaches

whether the property of one spouse will automatically become the

property of the other spouse.

4 **Please translate into English**

Die Parteien des Rechtsstreits, Kläger und Beklagter, betreten mit ihren Anwälten den Sitzungsraum. Weder die Juroren noch der Richter sind bereits
anwesend. Der Gerichtsdiener erscheint: *„Bitte erheben Sie sich!"* Der Richter und die Juroren betreten den Sitzungsraum. Der Kläger fordert in seiner
Klageschrift 30 Millionen US$ Strafschadensersatz. Er behauptet, durch ein
Medikament gesundheitliche Schäden erlitten zu haben, das im Unternehmen
des Beklagten hergestellt worden war. Der Beklagte bestreitet in seiner Klageerwiderung alle Behauptungen des Klägers. Die Juroren betrachten den Kläger. Er sieht wirklich elend aus. Die Beweisaufnahme beginnt. Die Anspruchsgrundlage ist *„negligence"*. Die Beweislast liegt beim Kläger. Nachdem der
letzte Zeuge des Klägers befragt worden ist, ruft der Beklagtenvertreter einen
medizinischen Sachverständigen auf. Er soll bestätigen, dass das Medikament
die behaupteten Schäden nicht ausgelöst haben kann. Am Ende der Verhandlung verliest der Sprecher der Jury ihren Spruch. Aufgrund der überwiegenden
Beweise befinden sie, dass der Beklagte dem Kläger für den von ihm vorgebrachten Schaden und für die erlittenen Schmerzen haftet. Die von der Jury
zugesprochene Entschädigungssumme ist US$ 30 Mio. Der Richter senkt die
Summe in seinem Urteil auf US$ 5 Mio.

The parties of the dispute, plaintiff and defendant, enter the court room

together with their attorneys. Neither the jury, nor the judge is present, yet.

The bailiff appears: "Please, rise!" The judge and the jury enter the court

room. In his complaint the plaintiff claims 30 million US$ of punitive

damages. He alleges that the drugs produced by the defendant's company

have caused him physical harm. In his answer the defendant denies every

allegation the plaintiff has made. The jurors look at the plaintiff. He looks

really miserable. The taking of evidence begins. The cause of action is

negligence. The burden of proof is with the plaintiff. After the last plaintiff's

witness has been questioned, the defendant's attorney calls a medical expert.
He wants him to confirm that the drug in question could not have caused
the harm alleged. At the end of the trial the spokesman of the jury reads the
verdict. Due to the preponderance of evidence they hold that the defendant
is liable for the damage put forward by the plaintiff and also for pain and
suffering. The amount for compensation, held by the jury, is 30 million US$.
In his judgment the judge cuts the sum to 5 million US$.

Fehler-Noten-Relation:

Fehler	Notenpunkte
0–1	18
2	17
3	16
4	15
5	14
6	13
7	12
8–9	11
10–11	10
12–13	9
14–15	8
16–17	7
18–19	6
20–22	5
23–25	4
26–35	3
36–45	2
46–50	1
>51	0

Mistakes: _____   Grade: _____

Abschlussklausur (S. 99)

1 Please fill in the gaps using the words in the list below

> apartment – assignee – assignment – assignor – borrower – contract of employment – employer – goods – interest – lease – lender – money – purchase price – rent – salary – sales contract – seller – services – tenant

contract	parties		objects	
sales contract	seller	buyer	goods	purchase price
loan	lender	borrower	money	interest
lease	landlord	tenant	apartment	rent
assignment (not a contract)	assignor	assignee	receivable	–
contract of employment	employer	employee	services	salary

2 Please fill in the gaps using the words below

> balances – branch – consisted – declared – defense – Executive – former – held – interests – justice – led – power – protect – pursuing – representing – separated

On July 4, 1776, following the American Revolution, the ____**former**____ colonies in the New World cut ties with England and ____**declared**____ their independence. The "Constitutional Convention" that ultimately produced today's U.S. Constitution was ____**held**____ in Philadelphia in 1787. The Convention ____**consisted**____ of 55 delegates, ____**representing**____ a wide variety of ____**interests**____ and backgrounds. George Washington ____**led**____ the Convention, whose members were determined to ____**protect**____ liberty, establish ____**justice**____ and provide for their common ____**defense**____. In ____**pursuing**____ these objectives, the delegates agreed that the government's ____**power**____ should be ____**separated**____ into three branches: Legislature, ____**Executive**____, and Judiciary. A system of checks and ____**balances**____ was created to prevent any single ____**branch**____ from becoming too powerful.

3 Bitte notieren Sie mit Hilfe der englischen Erklärungen die englischen Begriffe der gesuchten Rechtsgebiete.

Beispiel: Money collected by the government from the people without giving something in return is called taxes. There is an almost unlimited list of taxes, such as income tax, sales tax, value added tax, inheritance tax.

Area of law: **tax law**

1. contracts
2. legal history
3. antitrust
4. civil procedure
5. public international law
6. criminal law
7. law of succession/law of inheritance
8. constitutional law
9. environmental law
10. comparative law
11. family law
12. torts/delict
13. employment law
14. conflict of laws/private international law
15. property

4 Reading comprehension: Please read Exkurs 2 on page 112/113 twice and answer the following questions in full sentences. What are the differences, what are the similarities of ius commune and common law?

similarities of ius commune and common law:

effect: harmonization of law

source of law for the judiciary: secondary source for i.c./primary source for c.l.

one language   Latin for ius commune, English for common law

differences:

	ius commune	common law
Who?	scholars	practitioners (judges)
Where?	continental Europe	England
When?	application in wider parts of Europe basically at the end of 15th century	started 1154 with Henry II
How?	university to university; university to court	court to court
What?	Rules deriving to a high degree from the CIC	court decisions, "ratio decidendi" – precedents
Approach	academic, abstract, dogmatic	practical, pragmatic, "craftsmanship"

5 **Please translate into English**

Der Gerichtsdiener führt den Angeklagten auf seinen Platz. Er ist des Mordes ersten Grades angeklagt. Die 12 Juroren beobachten jede Bewegung. Der Bezirksstaatsanwalt erhebt sich. Er hat vor zwei Monaten gegen den Beklagten Anklage erhoben. Er beginnt damit, dem Angeklagten und der *Jury* die Anklageschrift vorzulesen. Nach dem Eröffnungsplädoyer des Bezirksstaatsanwalts hält der Verteidiger seinen Eröffnungsvortrag. Jede Seite ist fest entschlossen, den Fall für sich zu gewinnen. Die Verteidigung ruft ihren ersten Zeugen auf. Langsam geht der Zeuge zum Zeugenstand. Nun hat der Staatsanwalt die Gelegenheit zum Kreuzverhör. Doch darauf hat der Verteidiger den Zeugen schon vorbereitet. Sie haben tagelang mögliche Fragen des Staatsanwalts besprochen. Nichts sollte dem Zufall überlassen bleiben. Am Ende des Prozesses erklärt der Richter der *Jury* die Rechtslage, und die Juroren ziehen sich zu ihren Beratungen zurück. Nun ist es an ihnen zu entscheiden, ob die vorgebrachten Tatsachen und die Beweise genügen, um den Angeklagten schuldig zu sprechen. Ihnen ist klar, im Zweifel gilt die Vermutung, dass der Angeklagte unschuldig ist. Nur wenn sie alle ohne jeden vernünftigen Zweifel davon ausgehen, dass er das Verbrechen begangen hat, lautet ihr Urteilsspruch „schuldig".

The bailiff walks the defendant to his seat. He is charged with first-degree murder. The 12 jurors watch his every move. The district attorney rises. He brought charges against the defendant two months ago. He starts by reading the indictment to the defendant and the jury. After the DA's opening statement, the defense attorney presents his opening statement. Each party is focused on winning its case. The defense calls its first witness. Slowly the witness takes the stand. The district attorney then has the opportunity to cross-examine. The defense attorney has already prepared the witness for this situation. For days they have reviewed potential questions that the DA might pose. Nothing should be a surprise to the witness. At the end of the trial, the judge explains the law to the jury and the jurors retreat for deliberations. Now it is up to them to decide whether the facts and the evidence are convincing enough to find the defendant guilty. They know he is presumed to be innocent. The defendant will only be found guilty if they all believe beyond a reasonable doubt *that he has committed the crime.*

6 **Please add the respective English and German terms to the following amendments**

Amendment I: Congress shall make no law respecting an establishment of religion, or prohibiting the free exercise thereof; or abridging the freedom of speech, or of the press; or the right of the people peaceably to assemble, and to petition the Government for a redress of grievances.

freedom of speech – freedom of the press – ~~prohibition of the establishment of religion~~ – right to free exercise of religion – right to peaceably assemble – right to petition

Meinungsfreiheit – Petitionsrecht – Pressefreiheit – Religionsausübungsfreiheit – ~~Verbot der Gründung einer Staatsreligion~~ – Versammlungsfreiheit

English	German equivalent
prohibition of the establishment of religion	Verbot der Gründung einer Staatsreligion
right to free exercise of religion	Religionsausübungsfreiheit
freedom of speech	Meinungsfreiheit
freedom of the press	Pressefreiheit
right to peaceably assemble	Versammlungsfreiheit
right to petition	Petitionsrecht

Amendment VI: In all criminal prosecutions, the accused shall enjoy the right to a speedy and public trial, by an impartial jury of the State and district wherein the crime shall have been committed, which district shall have been previously ascertained by law, [...] and to have the Assistance of Counsel for his defence.

district of court shall be previously ascertained – right to a public trial – right to a speedy trial – right to an impartial jury – right to counsel for his defense

Beschleunigungsgrundsatz – existiert so nicht – Öffentlichkeitsgrundsatz – Recht auf Pflichtverteidiger – Teil des Grundsatzes des gesetzlichen Richters

English	German equivalent
right to a speedy trial	Beschleunigungsgrundsatz
right to a public trial	Öffentlichkeitsgrundsatz
right to an impartial jury	existiert so nicht
district of court shall be previously ascertained	Teil des Grundsatzes des gesetzlichen Richters
right to counsel for his defense	Recht auf Pflichtverteidiger

7 **Please fill in the gaps using the words in the list below**

> *actually – called – chattel – contracts – distinguish – divided – equals – immovable property – inheritance – intangible – lead – linked – movable property – patents – personal property – principle of separation and abstraction – property – real estate – tangible – things – unlike*

Property law is closely _____linked_____ to many other areas of law such as the law of _____contracts_____, the law of secured transactions, or the law of _____inheritance_____, the latter also _____called_____ law of succession. This link is even closer in common law legal systems than in German law because, _____unlike_____ in German law, in most common law legal systems there is no _____principle of separation and abstraction_____, which would separate and _____distinguish_____ between two different kinds of contracts: those that _____lead_____ to an obligation to transfer _____property_____, and those that _____actually_____ transfer the property. The law of property is also relevant for bankruptcy law. _____Things_____ are _____divided_____ into separate categories: There is _____movable property_____ and _____immovable property_____.

Movable property includes for example cars, clothes, chairs and tables, immovable property is pieces of land, also called _____real estate_____.

Both movable and immovable property have synonyms: movable property equals _____personal property_____, immovable property _____equals_____ real property. Movable property might be _____tangible_____ or _____intangible_____. Tangible movable property is called _____chattel_____. Examples for intangibles are _____patents_____.

8 **Please add the English equivalent**

Abtretung	assignment
Allgemeine Geschäftsbedingungen	standard terms, terms and conditions
anfechtbar	voidable
Angebot	offer
Anzahlung	down payment
Arbeitnehmer/in	employee
ausdrücklich	express
ausreichend, hinreichend	sufficient

bedeutend	significant
bei Erhalt der Ware	on receipt of the goods
Beklagte(r)	defendant
Besitz aufgeben	to relinquish possession
Besitzstörung	trespass
Betrug	fraud
Beweis	evidence
Bundesrecht	federal law
darlegen, vorschreiben	to set forth
Darlehen	loan
Darlehensnehmer/in	borrower
ehelicher Güterstand	matrimonial property
Einbruchdiebstahl	burglary
einen Vertrag schließen	to conclude a contract
einschränken	to abridge
Einwilligung	consent
Ergebnis	outcome
erwerben, erhalten	to obtain
etwas in Betracht ziehen	to take sth. into consideration
Federführung, Schirmherrschaft	auspices
gegen jmd. Anklage erheben	to bring charges against s.o.
Geldstrafe	fine
Gerichtsdiener/in	bailiff
gewährleisten, bereitstellen, beinhalten	to provide for
Gewährleistung(srecht)	warranty
Grundstück	piece of land
haftbar gemacht werden für	to be held liable for
Irrtum	mistake
jmd. in Untersuchungshaft nehmen	to take s.o. into custody
jmd. ins Kreuzverhör nehmen	to cross-examine s.o.
Kanzlei	law firm
Kindeswohl	the best interest and welfare of the child
Klageerwiderung	answer
Klageschrift	complaint
Laien	lay people
Nothilfe	defense of another

Querschnitt	cross section
rechtsprechende Gewalt	judiciary
Rechtsquelle	source of law
Rechtsstreit	dispute
rechtsverbindlich	binding
Richter/in	judge
Scheidung	divorce
Scheitern, Ausbleiben	failure
Schmerzensgeld	damages for pain and suffering
Sicherungsrecht	security interest
Sorgerecht	custody
Strafverfahren	criminal proceedings
Strafverteidiger/in	defense attorney
überzeugend	persuasive
ungeachtet	regardless of
ungerechtfertigte Bereicherung	unjust enrichment
Unterhalt	financial support
Unterhaltsverpflichtung	maintenance obligation
verhandeln	to negotiate
verklagt werden wegen	to be sued for
Verlassen, Imstichlassen	desertion
verletzen	to infringe, to violate, to breach
Verordnung	regulation
Versuch	attempt
Verwaltungsrecht	administrative law
Vollstreckung	enforcement
vorbringen	to put forth
vorsätzlich, absichtlich	intentional
Waren	goods
Wille, Absicht	intent
Zeuge, Zeugin	witness
Zivilklage, Zivilsache	civil action
zur Sache	on the merits
zusprechen	to grant

9 **Please translate into German**

Family law in most jurisdictions encompasses, at a minimum, the law of marriage, termination of marriage, matrimonial property, financial support, custody of children and adoption. Marriages can be terminated either by an annulment or a divorce. An annulment means that the marriage was void or voidable from the start and, therefore, it is treated as though it never existed. A divorce, on the other hand, is a legal dissolution of the relationship of husband and wife. In most states, a divorce will be granted on the basis of adultery, desertion or cruel treatment, among other things. A "no-fault" divorce will be granted if the parties agree to terminate the marriage due to irreconcilable differences. In some cases, the court will award alimony to one spouse – the money paid for the maintenance of a spouse, for a definite or indefinite period of time. Similarly, if the couple has children, the court may decide to award custody and child support to one of the parties. In determining the custody of the children, the court must decide what is in "the best interest and welfare" of the children.

Familienrecht umfasst in den meisten Rechtssystemen mindestens das Eherecht, die Beendigung von Ehen, Ehegüterrecht, Unterhalt, Sorgerecht für Kinder und Adoption. Ehen können entweder durch Annullierung oder durch Scheidung aufgelöst werden. Annullierung bedeutet, dass die Ehe von Beginn an unwirksam oder anfechtbar war und daher so behandelt wird, als hätte sie nie existiert. Eine Scheidung auf der anderen Seite ist die rechtliche Auflösung der Beziehung zwischen Ehemann und Ehefrau. In den meisten Staaten wird eine Scheidung unter anderem ausgesprochen auf der Grundlage von Ehebruch, Imstichlassen oder grausamer Behandlung. Eine verschuldensunabhängige Scheidung wird ausgesprochen, wenn die Parteien darüber einig sind, ihre Ehe aufgrund unüberbrückbarer Differenzen beenden zu wollen. In manchen Fällen wird das Gericht einem Ehegatten Unterhalt zusprechen – Geld für die Versorgung eines Ehegatten für eine bestimmte oder unbestimmte Zeit. Gleichermaßen kann das Gericht einer der Parteien das Sorgerecht und Kindesunterhalt zusprechen, wenn das Ehepaar Kinder hat. Bei der Bestimmung des Sorgerechts muss das Gericht entscheiden, was dem Kindeswohl entspricht.

10 **Please fill in the gaps using the words from the list below**

> *arrested – arson – attempt – burglary – consented – custody – defense –*
> *fraud – intimidation – misdemeanours – mistake – motives – murder –*
> *offenses – robbery – self-defense – shoplifting – source – suspects – takes –*
> *theft – trial – victim*

The area of criminal law is what every non-lawyer seems to be most interested in. It provides a _____ **source** _____ for many novels and movies. Which one of the _____ **suspects** _____ committed the crime? What were his _____ **motives** _____? Who was the _____ **victim** _____? Minor crimes are called _____ **offenses** _____, minor offenses are called _____ **misdemeanours** _____. Most of the time the suspect is _____ **arrested** _____ after he has accomplished the crime. But even the _____ **attempt** _____ to commit a crime can be punished. In certain cases the suspect can be taken into _____ **custody** _____ and put into jail until the end of his _____ **trial** _____, especially in serious and intentional crimes such as _____ **murder** _____, rape or _____ **arson** _____. A murder can be first-degree when it is committed in a particularly malicious way. Minor offenses are e.g. assault and battery, _____ **fraud** _____, defamation or _____ **theft** _____. A theft that is committed in a supermarket is called _____ **shoplifting** _____ and if a thief breaks into someone else's house in order to steal things it is called a _____ **burglary** _____. If violence or _____ **intimidation** _____ is used against a person while the offender _____ **takes** _____ away the person's property it is called _____ **robbery** _____. In his _____ **defense** _____ the suspect might allege that he acted in _____ **self-defense** _____ or defense of another, or that the victim _____ **consented** _____ to his conduct. Further, he may have acted in this certain way by _____ **mistake** _____.

11 **Please translate into German**

Most of the time the suspect is arrested after he has accomplished the crime. But already the attempt of a crime can be punished. In certain cases the suspect can be taken into custody and put into jail until the end of his trial, especially for serious and intentional crimes like murder, rape or arson.

Meistens wird der Verdächtige verhaftet, nachdem er die Tat vollendet hat.

Bereits der Versuch einer Straftat kann aber bestraft werden. In bestimmten

Fällen kann der Tatverdächtige in Untersuchungshaft genommen werden und bis zum Ende seiner Verhandlung ins Gefängnis kommen, vor allem bei schweren und vorsätzlichen Verbrechen wie Mord, Vergewaltigung oder Brandstiftung.

Fehler-Noten-Relation:

Fehler	Notenpunkte
0–2	18
3–4	17
5–6	16
7–8	15
9–10	14
11–12	13
13–14	12
15–16	11
17–18	10
19–20	9
21–23	8
24–26	7
27–29	6
30–32	5
33–35	4
36–40	3
41–45	2
46–50	1
>51	0

Mistakes: _____ Grade: _____

L. Literaturhinweise

Erfahrungsberichte

Australien

Heuser, LL.M. Studium in Down Under, JuS 1996, S. 478 ff.

Kanada

Bachmann, McGill-University, Montreal: Der L.L.M., der aus der Kälte kam, Jura 1996, S. 276 ff.

Blechschmidt, Wahlstation an der Deutsch-Kanadischen Industrie- und Handelskammer in Toronto, Jura 1995, S. 615 ff.

Broichhausen, Common Law – Erfahrung am Pazifik, Anwaltspraktikum in Vancouver, Jura 2002, S. 210 ff.

Gut, Studium an der Mc Gill University, Montréal, Jura 2001, S. 637 ff.

Lembke, Rechtsanwaltspraktikum in Toronto/Kanada – Tipps und Erfahrungen, JuS 1995, S. 948 ff.

Leonardy, Wahlstation im Native Law in Kanada, JuS 1995, S. 277 ff.

Menne, Französische Rechtskultur in Quebec, Jura 1996, S. 389 ff.

Neuseeland

Klein, Umweltrechtsstudium im Land der langen weißen Wolke, Jura 2001, S. 427 ff.

Südafrika

Häußler, Gute Hoffnung für die Republik am Kap – Die neue Verfassung Südafrikas, JA 1997, 995 ff.

Helfritz, Studienmöglichkeiten für deutsche Juristen in Südafrika, Jura 1996, S. 446 ff.

Link, Das Zentrum für Menschenrechte der Universität Pretoria, Jura 2005, S. 500 ff.

Maluch, Verwaltungsstation am deutschen Generalkonsulat in Kapstadt, JuS 1995, S. 565 ff.

USA

Balders, Forschungsaufenthalt an der Harvard Law School im Rahmen eines DAAD-Doktorandenkurzstipendiums, JuS 2000, S. 102 ff.

Bardo, Das LL.M.-Studium an der Yale Law School, JuS 1996, S. 85 ff.; *Buchner,* Studieren in Los Angeles, Jura 2004, S. 142.

Blinn, Studieren und arbeiten in den USA – ein praktischer Leitfaden, JuS 1992, S. 893 ff.

Breßler, Mediation und Negotiation an einer US-amerikanischen Law School, JuS 2000, S. 1141 ff.

Brose, Praktikum beim Office of the Public Defender, City and Country of San Francisco, Jura 1999, S. 557 ff.

Bungert, Auf Max Rheinsteins Spuren – LL.M.-Werdung an der University of Chicago Law School zwischen Economic Analysis of Law und Sears Tower, JuS 1993, S. 1072 ff.

Geis, Wahlstation in der Kanzlei Rowland & Partner in New York, Jura 2006, S. 798 f.

Gille, Auslandsstudium in den USA – ein Erfahrungsbericht von der University of Michigan Law School, Ann Arbor, Jura 2002, S. 500 ff.

Göthel/Sandmann, Deutsche Juristen in den USA – Studium und Alternativen, Jura 2000, S. 605 ff.

Harrer/Patschon, Das New York Bar Exam, JuS 1995, S. 757 ff.

Hartmann, Besser? Schlechter? – Anders. Anwaltspraktikum in Amerika, Jura 1997, S. 670 ff.

Hartmann, Das LL.M. in Comparative Law – Programm an der University of San Diego School of Law, Jura 1998, S. 558 ff.

Hartmann, Amerikanisches Recht und sein Studium in den USA. Seminar der Deutsch-Amerikanischen-Juristen-Vereinigung e.V., Jura 2001, S. 424 ff.

Hartmann, Das LL.M.-Studium an der University of Virginia School of Law, Jura 2003, S. 356 ff.

Heckmann, Praktikum bei der United Nations Association of the United States of America in New York, Jura 1997, S. 221 ff.

Herrmann, Philadelphia, here I come! – Ein Jahr zum LL.M.-Studium in Amerika, JuS 1999, S. 1036 ff.

Hingst, Wahlstation am Generalkonsulat der Bundesrepublik Deutschland in New York, Jura 2001, S. 208 ff.

Hürtig, Praktikum bei einer Anwaltskanzlei in Los Angeles, Jura 2001, S. 65 ff.

Kochinke/Wilske, USA Bewerbungsführer für Juristen, Deutsch-Amerikanische Juristen-Vereinigung e.V., Bonn 2003.

König, Praktikum am Superior Court of the District of Columbia, Washington D.C., USA, Jura 1998, S. 447.

Lagardère, Wahlstation im Office of the Public Defender in San Diego, Jura 2006, S. 879.

Leirer, Postgraduiertenstudium an der University of Georgia, JuS 1995, S. 375 ff.

Luis, Die Wahlstation für Rechtsreferendare beim Representative of German Industry and Trade in Washington D.C., Jura 1999, S. 278 ff.

Mayer, Internship in der Rechtsabteilung der UNO in New York, JuS 1995, S. 371 ff.

Menner, LL.M.-Programm an der University of Houston, Law Center, JuS 1994, S. 991 ff.

Müller, Auslandssemester bei den Vereinten Nationen in New York, JuS 1990, S. 336 ff.

Naether, Studienreise der Juristischen Fakultät der Martin-Luther-Universität in die USA, Jura 1997, S. 501 ff.

Ostermaier, Auslandspraktikum: Rechtsanwalt in Oakland/Kalifornien, Jura 1995, S. 500 ff.; *Peters,* Erfahrungsbericht über ein Praktikum bei einem Anwalt in Miami, Jura 2000, S. 222 ff.

Rademacher/Empt, LL.M. in International and Comparative Law am University of Iowa College of Law, Jura 2003, S. 141 ff.

Radu, Wahlstation in einer US-amerikanischen Anwaltskanzlei, JuS 1994, S. 815 ff.; dazu Anmerkung in: *Baudisch,* JuS 1994, S. 1088 ff.

Rakowski, Rechtslehre und -praxis in den USA: Wandel und Aussichten, JuS 2000, S. 525 ff.

Reimann, Vom Deutschen Staatsdiener zum Amerikanischen Anwalt, JuS 1994, S. 282 ff.

Rosenau, Sommerausflug ins anglo-amerikanische Recht, Jura 1995, S. 163 ff.

Ruprecht/Weber, I see, I forget. I hear, I forget. I do, I remember: National Model United Nations in New York, Jura 2001, S. 715 ff.

Schnutenhaus, ALICS-American Law Introductory Courses Saarbrücken, JuS 1991, S. 616 ff.

Schroeter, Der Willem C. Vis International Commercial Arbitration Moot – Herausforderung für Studenten mit Interesse am internationalen Wirtschaftsrecht, JuS 1996, S. 83 ff.

Schüürmann, Wahlstation bei der Representative For German Industry And Trade in Washington, DC., JuS 1991, S. 615 ff.

Sfiligoj, Wahlstation beim Office of the District Attorney in Sante Rose (Kalifornien), JuS 1990, S. 427 ff.

Troost, Einführung in das Rechtssystem der Vereinigten Staaten – Das Leiden-Amsterdam-Columbio-Summer Program 1996, JuS 1998, S. 285 ff.

Wolf, Praktische Studienzeit bei Tom Bolt & Associates, PC auf den US Virgin Islands, Jura 1997, S. 502 ff.

Vereinigtes Königreich

Becker, University of Cambridge – Summer School in English Legal Methods, JuS 1993, S. 439 ff.

Dassler, Wahlstation bei dem deutschen Generalkonsulat in Edinburgh, Jura 2000, S. 220 ff.

During, Auslandsstudium in Großbritannien – zugleich ein Erfahrungsbericht über zwei Semester als undergraduate an einer Law School in London, JuS 1997, S. 478 ff.

Eckhardt, Ein (akademisches) Jahr am University College London, Jura 1996, S. 501 ff.

Erwin, Praktikum bei einer internationalen Anwaltskanzlei in Frankfurt und London, Jura 1998, S. 166 ff.

Erwin, Auslandsstudium (M.Jur.) an der University of Oxford, JuS 2001, S. 1241 ff.

Franck, Ein akademisches Jahr am Law Department der London School of Economics and Political Science, Jura 2001, S. 207 ff.

Früchtl, Praktikumsbericht am Notariat Cheeswrights, London, Jura 2001, S. 860 ff.

Grammes, Wahlstation bei einem schottischen Rechtsanwalt, JuS 1995, S. 855 ff.

Heckelmann, Masterfahndung, Entscheidungshilfen zum LL.M.-Studium in den USA, Jura 2007, S. 637 f.

Hingst, Die Zulassung als „Solicitor in England und Wales", Jura 2004, S. 716 ff.

Jasper, LL.M.-Studium in London, JuS 1990, S. 686 ff.

Kirchner, Die Summer School in English Legal Methods der Faculty of Law sowie des Board of Continuing Education der University of Cambridge, Jura 2001, S. 138 ff.

Koch, Anwaltspraktikum bei einer barristers' chamber in Leeds, Jura 1995, S. 165 ff.

Lauchs, Zwischen Whiskey und Kilt – Der European Young Lawyers Scheme des British Council in Edinburgh, Jura 2002, S. 424 ff.

Lützeler, Legal studies at coleg prifysgol cymru, aberystwyth – Erfahrungen und Informationen über das Studium an einer walisischen Universität, JuS 1993, S. 176 ff.

Menger, Wahlstation im House of Commons, London, JuS 1992, S. 448 ff.

Modlmayr/Müller, Cross Border LL.M. „Human Rights and Criminal Justice" an der Queen's University Belfast und der National University of Ireland Galway, Jura 2005, S.155 ff.

Multerer, Ferienkurs „English for Law" an der Universität von St. Andrews, Jura 1996, S. 277 ff.

Reimann, The Edinburgh Experience – More Than a Degree, Jura 1995, S. 108 ff.

Reimnitz, Akademisches Jahr 2002/2003 an der juristischen Fakultät des University College London als "full time student" unterstützt von Erasmus/Socrates und der Studienstiftung des deutschen Volkes, Jura 2004, S.69 ff.

Rosenau, Sommerausflug ins anglo-amerikanische Recht, Jura 1995, S. 163 ff.

Rösler, Studium an einer London School of Economics and Political Science (LSE) und praktische Studienzeit bei der Verwaltung eines Londoner Stadtteils, JuS 1997, S. 285 ff.

Ruttig, In der Hauptstadt Schottlands, Jura 1997, S. 110 ff.

Siebert, Das Studium zum „Certificate of Higher Education in Common Law" an der Norwich School, University of East Anglia (UEA), Jura 2004, S. 427 f.

Talmon, LL.M.-Studium an der University of Cambridge (Wolfson College) nicht nur für Referendare, JuS 1991, S. 522 ff.

Voigt, Der LL.M. und andere Postgraduierten-Qualifikationen im Vergleich, Jura 2007, S. 558 ff.

Winkler, LL.M.-Studium International and European Legal Studies an der University of Durham, Großbritannien, Jura 2001, S. 349 ff.; Neuer Aufbaustudiengang – Master in British Studies (M.B.S.), Jura 1999, S. 556 ff. *Website:* http://www2.rz.hu-berlin.de/gbz

Zum Recht anglo-amerikanischer Rechtssysteme (auf Deutsch)

Länderübergreifend

Blumenwitz, Einführung in das anglo-amerikanische Recht, 7. Auflage (2003)

Byrd, Introduction to Anglo-American Law & Language, 2. Auflage (2001)

Dietl/Lorenz, Wörterbuch für Recht, Wirtschaft und Politik, Band I, 6. Auflage (2000)

Dietl/Lorenz, Wörterbuch für Recht, Wirtschaft und Politik, Band II, 5. Auflage (2005)

Flory/Froschauer, Grundwortschatz der Rechtssprache (deutsch/englisch – englisch/deutsch), 3. Auflage (2003).

Australien

Kment, Die erste „Bill of Rights" Australiens: „Human Rights Act 2004", JA 2005, S. 399 ff.

USA

Dubber, Einführung in das US-amerikanische Strafrecht (2005).

Göthel, Internationales Vertragsrecht der USA (2002).

Hay, US-Amerikanisches Recht, 3. Auflage (2005).

Oellers, Die Amerikanische Unabhängigkeitserklärung vom 4.7.1776, JuS 1993, S. 799 ff.

Reimann, Einführung in das US-amerikanische Privatrecht, 2. Auflage (2004).

Schack, Einführung in das US-amerikanische Zivilprozessrecht, 3. Auflage (2003).

Schmitz, Notwendiger Verbraucherschutz oder übertriebene Strafe? – Schadenersatzzahlungen in den USA, JuS 1999, S. 941 ff.

Schubert, Die Allzuständigkeit US-amerikanischer Gerichte, Jura 2003, S. 522 ff.

Waibel, Junges Volk mit alter Verfassung – Entstehung und Inhalt der amerikanischen Verfassung von 1787, JuS 2001, S. 1048 ff.

Vereinigtes Königreich

Dörfert, How to conclude a contract – Bemerkungen zum Vertragsschluss nach deutschem und englischem Recht, JA 1998, 435 ff.

Fenton, The Human Rights Act of the United Kingdom, Jura 2000, S. 330 ff.

Graf von Bernstorff, Einführung in das englische Recht, 3. Auflage 2005.

Heberer, Einführung in das englische Rechtssystem (2002), S. 57 ff.

Henry/Pike, English law and legal language: Introduction (2006).

Henry/Pike, English law and legal language: Criminal Law (2006).

Kleinschmidt, Unilateral contract und einseitiges Versprechen, Jura 2007, S. 249 ff.

Riesenhuber, Englisches Restitutionsrecht – in einer Nussschale, Jura 2002, S. 657 ff.

Wörlen, Introduction to English Civil Law for German-Speaking Lawyers and Law Students, 3. Auflage (2005).

Zum Recht anglo-amerikanischer Rechtssysteme (auf Englisch)

USA

Burnham, Introduction to the Law and Legal System of the United States, 4. Auflage (2006).

Farnsworth, An Introduction to the Legal System of the United States, 3. Auflage (1999).

Hay, Law of the United States, 2. Auflage (2005).

M. Nützliche Websites

General useful websites

German-English/English-German dictionary: http://dict.leo.org
German-English/English-German dictionary: http://www.dict.cc
English legal dictionary: http://dictionary.law.com

Informationen zum Auslandsstudium: http://www.juracafe.de/ausbildung/studium/ausland.htm
Informationen zum LL.M.-Studium weltweit: http://www.llm-guide.com/

Australia

Australia legal news: http://scaleplus.law.gov.au/
Australian Law on the internet: http://www.nla.gov.au/oz/law.html
Australia information on legal education: http://jurist.law.mq.edu.au
Linksammlung: http://www.austlii.edu.au/links/215.html

Canada

Canada non-legal news: http://www.globeandmail.com and http://www.canada.com/nationalpost/
Canada legal news and legal information: http://jurist.law.utoronto.ca
Parliament and legislation of Canada: http://www.parl.gc.ca

India

India non-legal news: http://www.timesofindia.com and http://www.expressindia.com
India legal news: http://www.indlaw.com and http://www.legalserviceindia.com/news/

Namibia

Namibia legal information: http://www.lac.org.na/laws/lawlinks.htm
Namibian Constitution: http://www.orusovo.com/namcon

New Zealand

New Zealand non-legal news: http://www.dompost.co.nz and http://www.nzherald.co.nz
New Zealand legislation: http://www.knowledge-basket.co.nz/tkbgp/welcome.html

Nigeria

Nigerian laws on the internet: http://www.nigeria-law.org/LFNMainPage.htm

South Africa

South Africa general information: http://www.polity.org.za/
South Africa legal information: http://www.washlaw.edu/forint/africa/soaf.html
South-African Constitution: http://www.concourt.gov.za/site/theconstitution/english.pdf
South Africa law firms: http://www.hg.org/firms-southafrica.html

United Kingdom

UK legislation: http://www.lexadin.nl/wlg/legis/nofr/eur/lxweuk.htm
UK Acts of Parliament: http://www.netlawman.co.uk/acts-of-parliament.php
UK news: http://www.timesonline.co.uk
UK and Ireland, information on LL.M.: http://www.llm-guide.com/uk-ireland
Legal resources for lawyers: http://www.venables.co.uk/sites.htm
Public and local Acts: http://www.hmso.gov.uk/acts.htm

United States

U.S. non-legal news: http://www.nytimes.com and http://www.washingtonpost.com
U.S. legal news and legal information: http://www.findlaw.com
U.S. Constitution auf Englisch: http://www.law.cornell.edu/constitution/constitution.text.html
U.S. Constitution auf Deutsch: http://usa.usembassy.de/etexts/gov/gov-constitiond.pdf
U.S. Supreme Court landmark decisions: http://www.constitution.org/ussc/ussc deci.htm
U.S. law schools information on LL.M.: http://www.llm-guide.com/usa

(Stand: 20.8.2007)

N. Vokabelliste

I. Englisch – Deutsch

A

abbreviation	Abkürzung
abduction	Entführung
abolish, to	abschaffen
abortion	Abtreibung
abridge, to	einschränken
accept an offer, to	ein Angebot annehmen
acceptance	Annahme
accidental	zufällig
accomplice	Mittäter/in
accomplished	vollendet
according to	gemäß, nach
accusation	Anklagepunkt, Anschuldigung
accuse, to	anklagen (materiell)
accused	Angeschuldigte(r)
achieve the best outcome, to	das beste Ergebnis erzielen
acknowledge, to	anerkennen
acquire, to	erwerben
acquisition	Erwerb
acquittal	Freispruch
act	aktives Tun, Gesetz
act, to	handeln
actual damage	tatsächlicher Schaden
address, to	*hier:* beinhalten
administrative law	Verwaltungsrecht
admissible	zulässig
adopt, to	annehmen, rezipieren; adoptieren
adoption	Adoption
adoptive parents	Adoptiveltern
adultery	Ehebruch
adversarial system	*dem common law Zivil- und Strafprozess zugrunde liegendes Prinzip*
advice	Rat
advocate	*schottischer, süd-afrikanischer oder namibischer Anwalt, der die Zulassung zu einem höheren Gericht hat*
affidavit	eidesstattliche Versicherung
agency	Stellvertretung
agent	Stellvertreter/in
aggravated	schwerer/e/es

agree on, to	sich einigen über, einverstanden sein mit
agreement	Einigung, Vereinbarung
alimony	Unterhalt(szahlungen) für den Ehegatten
allegation	Behauptung
allege, to	behaupten
alter, to	verändern
amend, to	ändern (ein Gesetz, einen Vertrag)
amendment	Verfassungszusatz
amendment of a statute	Gesetzesänderung
amount in controversy	Streitwert
analogy	Analogie
anchor, to	verankern
annulment	Annullierung
answer	Klageerwiderung
antitrust (law)	Kartellrecht
appeal	Berufung
appear before court, to	vor Gericht erscheinen
applicability	Anwendbarkeit
application	Bewerbung, Anwendung
apply to, to	anwendbar sein auf
apply, to	anwenden
appoint, to	ernennen, benennen
appointment	Termin
approval	Genehmigung
approve, to	billigen, zustimmen, genehmigen
arbitrary	willkürlich
arbitration	Schiedsgerichtsbarkeit
arbitration proceedings	Schiedsverfahren
area of law	Rechtsgebiet
argument	Argument
arise, to	entstehen, aufkommen
armed	bewaffnet
arms	Waffen
arrest someone, to	jemanden verhaften
arrest warrant	Haftbefehl
arson	Brandstiftung
arsonist	Brandstifter/in
as a result	im Ergebnis, demzufolge, daher
as to …	was … betrifft
assassination	Attentat
assault	Körperverletzung
assemble, to	versammeln
asset	Vermögensgegenstand
assets	Vermögen
assignable	abtretbar
assignee	Zessionar/in
assignment	Abtretung
assignor	Zedent/in
associate	*angestellter Anwalt einer US-Kanzlei*
association	Verein
assume, to	vermuten

attach, to	anhängen
attempt	Versuch
attorney	*US-amerikanischer oder süd-afrikanischer Anwalt, der die Zulassung zu einem Gericht erster Instanz hat*
auction	Versteigerung
auspices	Federführung, Schirmherrschaft
authority	Behörde
authorization	Vollmacht
authorize, to	ermächtigen
available	erreichbar
award, to	zusprechen

B

back-payment	Rückzahlung
bail	Kaution, Sicherheitsleistung
bailiff	Gerichtsdiener/in
ballpen	Kugelschreiber
banking law	Bankrecht
bankruptcy law	Insolvenzrecht
barrister	*englischer Anwalt, der den Mandanten vor Gericht vertritt*
basic right	Grundrecht
battery	Körperverletzung
be based on, to	auf etwas beruhen, basieren auf
be caught red-handed, to	auf frischer Tat ertappt werden
be charged with, to	etwas angeklagt sein
be composed of, to	zusammengesetzt sein aus
be confronted with, to	*hier:* gegenübergestellt werden
be considered, to	betrachtet werden
be divided, to	unterteilt sein
be entitled to, to	einen Anspruch haben auf
be governed by, to	geregelt sein durch
be held liable, to	haftbar gemacht werden für
be liable for, to	haftbar sein für
be obliged, to	verpflichtet sein
be on strike, to	streiken
be questioned, to	befragt werden
be reserved to, to	vorbehalten sein
be subject to something, to	etwas unterliegen
be sued for, to	verklagt werden wegen/auf
beneficiary	Begünstigte(r)
benefit	Nutzen
beyond a reasonable doubt	über jeden vernünftigen Zweifel hinaus *(Maßstab für eine Verurteilung im Strafprozess des common law)*
bias	befangen
bill	Gesetzentwurf
binding	bindend, rechtsverbindlich
bona fide purchase	gutgläubiger Erwerb
borrower	Darlehensnehmer/in

both ... and ...	sowohl ... als auch ...
branch	Niederlassung
breach of contract	Vertragsverletzung
breach, to	verletzen
bring an action, to	Klage erheben
bring charges against s.o., to	anklagen (formell), gegen jemanden Anklage erheben
burden of proof	Beweislast
burglar	Einbrecher/in
burglary	Einbruchdiebstahl
business law	Wirtschaftsrecht
business partner	Geschäftspartner/in
buy, to	kaufen
buyer	Käufer/in
by means of	mittels

C

call, to	aufrufen
cancel, to	kündigen
capital punishment	Todesstrafe
case law	Fallrecht, Rechtsprechung
causation	Kausalität
cause, to	verursachen
century	Jahrhundert
challenge, to	ablehnen (prozessual), eine Einrede erheben gegen
chancellor	Kanzler/in
charge, to	berechnen, in Rechnung stellen
chattel	körperlicher Gegenstand
child support	Kindesunterhalt
choice of court agreement	Gerichtsstandsvereinbarung
choice of law	Rechtswahl
circulate, to	in Umlauf geben, herumreichen
circumstances	Umstände
citizen	Bürger/in
civil action	Zivilklage, Zivilsache
Civil Code	Bürgerliches Gesetzbuch
civil procedure	Zivilprozessrecht
civil right	Bürgerrecht
civil war	Bürgerkrieg
claim, to	fordern
class action	Sammelklage
clerk	*Assistent/in des Richters in den USA*
client	Mandant/in
code of civil procedure	Zivilprozessordnung
coercion	Zwang
collateral	Sicherungsgut
collective agreement	Tarifvertrag
come into force, to	in Kraft treten
commentary	Kommentar
commerce	Handel

commercial law	Wirtschaftsrecht
commission	Provision
commit, to	begehen, verüben
community of property	Gütergemeinschaft
company	Gesellschaft, Unternehmen
company law	Gesellschaftsrecht
comparative law	Rechtsvergleichung
compensate, to	entschädigen
compensation	Entschädigung
compensatory damages	kompensatorischer Schadensersatz
competition	Wettbewerb
complaint	Klageschrift
complete, to	fertigstellen
completion	Beendigung
compulsory	zwingend
concept	Konzept
conclude a contract, to	einen Vertrag schließen
conclusion of a contract	Vertragsschluss
concurrent jurisdiction	konkurrierende Zuständigkeit
condition	Zustand, Bedingung
conditional	bedingt
conduct	Verhalten
confer on, to	jm. etwas übertragen
confess, to	gestehen
confession	Geständnis
confirm, to	bestätigen
conflict of laws	Internationales Privatrecht
connecting factor	Anknüpfungspunkt (im IPR)
consent	Einwilligung
consider, to	betrachten, erachten
consist of, to	bestehen aus
constitution	Verfassung
constitutional law	Verfassungsrecht
construction	Auslegung
construe, to	auslegen
consult, to	zu Rate ziehen
consumer	Verbraucher/in
consumer protection	Verbraucherschutz
content	Inhalt
contract	Vertrag
contract for the sale of land	Grundstückskaufvertrag
contracts	Vertragsrecht
contractual	vertraglich
contrary to public policy	sittenwidrig
contributory negligence	Mitverschulden
controversy	Streitigkeit
convey, to	Eigentum an einem Grundstück übertragen
conveyancer	*Urkundsperson bei der Übertragung des Eigentums an einem Grundstück*
convict	Strafgefangener
convince, to	überzeugen

copyright law	Urheberrecht
cornerstone	Eckpfeiler
council	Rat
counsel	*namibischer Anwalt, der die Zulassung zu einem Gericht erster Instanz hat*
counter claim	Widerklage, Gegenforderung
court	Gericht
court decision	Gerichtsentscheidung
court fees	Gerichtskosten
court of first instance	Gericht erster Instanz
court room	Gerichtssaal
create, to	schaffen, erschaffen
creditor	Gläubiger/in
crime	Verbrechen; Delikt
criminal law	Strafrecht
criminal procedure	Strafprozessrecht
criminal proceeding	Strafverfahren
criminal prosecution	Strafverfolgung; Strafverfahren
criminology	Kriminologie
cross section	Querschnitt
cross-examine, to	jmd. ins Kreuzverhör nehmen
custody	Haft, Gewahrsam, Sorgerecht
customary law	Gewohnheitsrecht
customer	Kunde, Kundin
cut ties with, to	Verbindungen abbrechen zu

D

damage	Schaden
damages	Schadensersatz
damages for pain and suffering	Schmerzensgeld
data	Daten, Angaben
deadline	Fristende
dealer	Händler/in
death penalty	Todesstrafe
death sentence	Todesurteil
debt	Schuld
debtor	Schuldner/in
deceased	Erblasser
decision	Entscheidung
decision-making power	Entscheidungsbefugnis
declaration	Erklärung
Declaration of Independence	Unabhängigkeitserklärung
declare, to	erklären
deem, to	halten für, vermuten
defamation	Beleidigung
default	Verzug
default judgment	Versäumnisurteil
defective	fehlerhaft, mangelhaft
defective product	fehlerhaftes Produkt
defendant	Angeklagter, Beklagter
defense	Einwendung, Einrede; Verteidigung

defense attorney	Strafverteidiger/in
defense of another	Nothilfe
definite	begrenzt
degree	Grad
delay	Verzug
delegate	Delegierte(r), Abgeordnete(r)
delegate to, to	delegieren, übertragen
deliberation	Beratung
delict	Delikt, Deliktsrecht
deliver, to	liefern
demand	Forderung
deny, to	bestreiten, verweigern, vorenthalten
deposit	Hinterlegung, Kaution (*im Mietrecht*)
deposition	Zeugenaussage
deprive someone of sth., to	jemandem etwas entziehen, vorenthalten
derive from, to	stammen von, sich ableiten von
descendent	Abkömmling
desertion	Verlassen, im Stich lassen
desk	Schreibtisch
determined, to be	entschlossen sein
deterrence	Abschreckung
deviate from, to	abweichen von
differ, to	sich unterscheiden
diligence	Sorgfalt
disclose, to	offenlegen
discover, to	entdecken
discretion	Ermessen
dismiss an action, to	eine Klage abweisen
dispossession	Besitzentziehung
dispute	Rechtsstreit, Streitigkeit
dissolution	Auflösung
dissolve, to	auflösen
distinct	unterschiedlicher/e/es
district	Bezirk
district attorney (DA)	Bezirksstaatsanwalt
divide, to	aufteilen
divorce	Scheidung
docket number	Aktenzeichen
doctrine	Schrifttum, Literatur
document	Urkunde
domicile	Wohnsitz
down payment	Anzahlung
draft	Entwurf
draw a distinction, to	unterscheiden
due	fällig
due to	aufgrund, wegen
duly convicted	rechtmäßig verurteilt (strafrechtlich)
duty of care	Sorgfaltspflicht
duty	Pflicht

E

E.C. law	Europarecht
e.g. (exempli gratia)	z.B. (zum Beispiel)
elect, to	wählen
eligible	wählbar
employee	Arbeitnehmer/in
employer	Arbeitgeber/in
employment contract	Arbeitsvertrag
employment law	Individualarbeitsrecht
enact, to	ein Gesetz erlassen
encompass, to	umfassen
enforce, to	vollstrecken
enforcement	Vollstreckung
engagement	Verlobung
enjoy a right, to	ein Recht genießen
ensure, to	sichern, absichern, sicherstellen
enter into a contract, to	einen Vertrag schließen
enter into effect, to	in Kraft treten
entirely	völlig, gänzlich
entry into force	Inkrafttreten
envelope	Umschlag
environmental law	Umweltrecht
equivalent	Entsprechung, Pendant
eraser	Radiergummi
error	Irrtum
essential	wesentlich
establish, to	schaffen, gründen
establishment	Errichtung, Gründung
estate	Nachlass, Vermögen
et al.	u.a. (und andere)
et seq.	ff. (folgende)
evaluate, to	bewerten
evidence	Beweis
ex officio	von Amts wegen
examine, to	vernehmen, befragen
except	außer
excessive	unverhältnismäßig hoch
exclusive jurisdiction	ausschließliche Zuständigkeit
executive power	ausführende Gewalt
exercise, to	ausüben
expenses	Aufwendungen
expert witness	Sachverständige(r)
express(ly)	ausdrücklich
express, to	zum Ausdruck bringen, ausdrücken
extension	Durchwahl
extradition	Auslieferung

F

fact	(bewiesene) Tatsache
factoring	Forderungskauf

facts (of the case)	Sachverhalt
failure	Scheitern, Ausbleiben
family law	Familienrecht
fault	Verschulden
fault-based liability	verschuldensabhängige Haftung
favourable	günstig
federal law	Bundesrecht
fee	Gebühr
felon	Vorbestrafte(r)
file	Akte
file a law suit, to	Klage erheben
final	endgültig
financial support	Unterhalt
find someone guilty, to	jemanden für schuldig befinden
find, to	befinden
fine	Geldstrafe
first-degree	schwer
focus on, to	sich konzentrieren auf
folder	Schnellhefter
Folgeschaden	consequential damage
follow a view, to	einer Ansicht folgen
forced heirship	Pflichtteil
foreseeability	Vorhersehbarkeit
forfeit a right, to	ein Recht verwirken
forfeiture	Verwirkung
formation of a contract	Vertragsschluss
former	erstgenannter/e/es
foundation	Stiftung, Gründung
founding fathers	Gründerväter
framework	Rahmen
fraud	arglistige Täuschung, Betrug, Täuschung, Arglist
fraudulent	arglistig, betrügerisch
free exercise	freie Ausübung
freedom	Freiheit
freedom of religion	Religionsfreiheit
freedom of speech	Redefreiheit
freedom of the press	Pressefreiheit
frustration	Vereitelung
fundamental right	Grundrecht

G

gain possession, to	Besitz erlangen
general part	Allgemeiner Teil
gift	Schenkung
goal	Ziel
good faith	Treu und Glauben
goods	Waren
govern, to	regieren, regeln
government	Regierung, Staat
grant, to	erteilen, zusprechen

gross negligence	grobe Fahrlässigkeit
guarantee, to	garantieren

H

habitual residence	gewöhnlicher Aufenthalt
hard drive	Festplatte
harm	Schaden, Verletzung
hearing	Anhörung
heir	Erbe
high treason	Hochverrat
highlighter	Textmarker
hold a convention, to	eine Versammlung abhalten
hold the line, to	am Apparat bleiben
hold, to	befinden
hole punch	Locher
homicide	Mord
hornbook	Lehrbuch
however	aber, jedoch
human right	Menschenrecht
husband	Ehemann
hybrid legal system	hybrides Rechtssystem

I

i.e. (id est = that is)	d.h. (das heißt)
immigrant	Einwanderer, Einwanderin
immovable property	unbewegliche Sachen
impartial	unparteiisch
impediment	Hindernis (rechtliches)
implied	konkludent, stillschweigend
impose, to	auferlegen
in addition	darüber hinaus, zusätzlich
in an effort to do sth.	in dem Bestreben etw. zu tun
in comparison to	im Vergleich zu
in compliance with	in Übereinstimmung mit
in his defense	zu seiner Verteidigung
in his favour	zu seinen Gunsten
in order to	um zu
in person	persönlich
in practice	in der Praxis
in question	fragliche
in the broad sense	im weiten Sinn
in the following	im Folgenden
in the narrow sense	im engen Sinn
in writing	schriftlich
inadmissible	unzulässig
include, to	beinhalten
incorporate, to	umfassen, verbinden
increase, to	ansteigen, sich erhöhen
indefinite	unbegrenzt
independence	Unabhängigkeit

independent	unabhängig
indictment	Anklageschrift
individual	einzelner/e/es
inevitable	unvermeidbar
inflict punishment, to	Strafe verhängen
influence, to	beeinflussen
infringe, to	verletzen
inheritance law	Erbrecht
injunction	einstweilige Verfügung
injustice	Ungerechtigkeit
ink	Tinte
inquisitorial system	*dem civil law-Zivil- und Strafprozess zugrundeliegendes Prinzip*
insolvent	zahlungsunfähig
instalment	Rate
instance	Fall, Umstand
instead	stattdessen
instruction	Weisung
insurance law	Versicherungsrecht
intangible property	unkörperliche Gegenstände
intellectual property	Gewerblicher Rechtsschutz
intent	Wille, Absicht
intention	Vorsatz, Absicht
intentional	vorsätzlich, absichtlich
interest	Zinsen
interest rate	Zinssatz
interfere with, to	stören, beeinträchtigen
international agreement	internationales Übereinkommen
international convention	internationale Konvention
international jurisdiction	internationale Zuständigkeit (eines Gerichts)
international treaty	internationaler Vertrag, Staatsvertrag
internship	Praktikum
interpret, to	auslegen
interpretation	Auslegung
interrogation	Befragung, Verhör
interview	Bewerbungsgespräch
intestate succession	gesetzliche Erbfolge
introduce, to	einführen
investigation	Ermittlungen
invitation to make an offer	invitatio ad offerendum
involuntary manslaughter	fahrlässige Tötung
involuntary servitude	unfreiwillige Dienste, Zwangsarbeit
irrebuttable	unwiderlegbar
irreconcilable	unüberbrückbar
issue a document, to	ein Dokument ausstellen

J

jail	Gefängnis
judge	Richter
judge-made law	Richterrecht

judgment	Urteil
judicial decision	Gerichtsentscheidung
judiciary	Judikative, rechtsprechende Gewalt
jurisdiction	Gerichtsbezirk i.w.S., Kompetenz-bereich, Zuständigkeit
juror	Geschworener
jury trial	Geschworenenverhandlung
just	gerecht
justice	Richter an einem obersten Gericht, Gerechtigkeit, Rechtsstaat
justification	Rechtfertigung
justify, to	rechtfertigen

L

labo(u)r law	Kollektives Arbeitsrecht
landlady	Vermieterin
landlord	Vermieter
landmark decision	Grundsatzentscheidung
latter	letztgenannter/e/es
law	Recht, Gesetz
law (review) article	juristischer Aufsatz
law firm	Kanzlei
law journal	juristische Zeitschrift
law of obligations	Schuldrecht
law of secured transactions	Kreditsicherungsrecht
law of succession	Erbrecht
law review	juristische Zeitschrift
law school	*entspricht der Juristischen Fakultät einer deutschen Universität*
lawful	rechtmäßig
lawfulness	Rechtmäßigkeit
lawyer	Jurist; Anwalt
lay people	Laien
lease	Mietvertrag
lease, to	mieten
legal aid	Prozesskostenhilfe
legal assistance	Rechtsbeistand
legal basis	rechtliche Grundlage, Rechtsgrundlage
legal capacity	Geschäftsfähigkeit
legal department	Rechtsabteilung
legal dictionary	Rechtswörterbuch
legal history	Rechtsgeschichte
legal person	juristische Person
legal philosophy	Rechtsphilosophie
legal problem	rechtliches Problem
legal relationship	Rechtsverhältnis
legal situation	Rechtslage
legal system	Rechtssystem
legal tradition	Rechtskreis, Rechtstradition
legal training	Praktikum
legislative act	Akt der Gesetzgebung

legislative body	Gesetzgebungsorgan
legislative power	Gesetzgebungsgewalt
legislator	Gesetzgeber
legislature	Gesetzgebung
legitimacy	Rechtmäßigkeit
legitimate	rechtmäßig
lender	Darlehensgeber/in
liberty	Freiheit
limitation	Einschränkung
limited	beschränkt
lis pendens	Rechtshängigkeit
litigate, to	prozessieren
litigation	Prozess, Rechtsstreit
loan	Darlehen; Leihe
loss	Schaden
loss of profit	entgangener Gewinn
lower court	unteres Gericht

M

maintenance	Lebensunterhalt, Unterhalt
maintenance obligation	Unterhaltsverpflichtung
majority	Volljährigkeit
make a contract, to	einen Vertrag schließen
make an offer, to	ein Angebot machen
malicious	böswillig, heimtückisch
management	Geschäftsleitung
managing director	Geschäftsführer/in
mandatory	zwingend
manslaughter	Mord, Totschlag
manufacturer	Hersteller/in
marriage	Ehe
marriage contract	Ehevertrag
matrimonial property	ehelicher Güterstand
maximize, to	maximieren
may	kann
may not	darf nicht
means	Mittel
measure	Maßnahme
medical expert	medizinischer Sachverständiger
meeting	Sitzung
member	Mitglied
Member State	Mitgliedstaat
memo	Aktennotiz
mercantile law	Handelsrecht
merger	Fusion
minor	Minderjährige(r)
minority	Minderjährigkeit
misdemeano(u)r	minderes Vergehen, Ordnungswidrigkeit
misrepresentation	Falschbehauptung
mistake	Irrtum (*strafrechtlich und zivilrechtlich*)

money laundering	Geldwäsche
mortgage	Hypothek
motion	Antrag (formell)
movable property	bewegliche Sachen
murder	Mord
murderer	Mörder/in
mutual	gegenseitig

N

natural person	natürliche Person
necessity	Notstand
negligence	Fahrlässigkeit
negligent	fahrlässig
negotiate, to	verhandeln
negotiation	Verhandlung
nevertheless	trotzdem, nichtsdestotrotz
non-contractual	außervertraglich
non-lawyer	Nichtjurist
non-performance	Nichterfüllung
notary	Notar/in
note	Nachricht
notepad	Notizblock
notion	Begriff, Konzept
null and void	nichtig

O

oath	Eid
objection	Einspruch
objective	Ziel
obligation	Verpflichtung, Pflicht
obtain, to	erwerben, erhalten
occur, to	geschehen, sich ereignen
offender	Täter/in
offense	Vergehen; Delikt
offer	Angebot
offer, to	anbieten
offeree	Annehmende(r)
offeror	Anbietende(r)
office supply	Bürobedarf, Bürogegenstände
omission	Unterlassen
on account of	wegen
on credit	auf Kredit
on receipt of the goods	bei Erhalt der Ware
on the merits	zur Sache
opening statement	Eröffnungsplädoyer
orally	mündlich
outcome	Ergebnis
over the course of	im Verlauf von
overtime	Überstunden
owe something, to	etwas schulden

owner	Eigentümer/in
ownership	Eigentum

P

paperclip	Büroklammer
parental responsibility	elterliche Verantwortung
particular	besonders, speziell
partner	*Anwalt, der Teilhaber einer Kanzlei ist*
party	Streitpartei, Vertragspartei
pass an act, to	ein Gesetz erlassen, verabschieden
pass s.o. on to s.b., to	jemanden weiterleiten an
passing of risk	Gefahrübergang
passing of title	Eigentumsübergang
patent law	Patentrecht
paternity	Vaterschaft
pay, to	zahlen
payment	Zahlung
peaceably	friedlich
pencil	Bleistift
pencil sharpener	Spitzer
people	Volk
perjury	Meineid
permission	Erlaubnis
permit	erlauben, gestatten
persecute, to	verfolgen
personal property	bewegliche Sachen
persuasive	überzeugend
physical harm	körperliche Schäden
piece of land	Grundstück
place of business	Niederlassung
plaintiff	Kläger/in
pleadings	Schriftsätze
pledge	Pfand
population	Bevölkerung
positive law	gesetztes Recht
possession	Besitz
possessor	Besitzer/in
postpone	vertagen
power	Macht, Befugnis
power of attorney	Vollmacht
practitioner	Praktiker/in
precedent	Präzedenzfall
predominantly	überwiegend
preferable	vorzugswürdig
preliminary proceedings	Vorverfahren
prenuptial agreement	Ehevertrag
preponderance of evidence	überwiegende Beweise/Beweislage
present, to	vortragen, vorlegen
preserve, to	bewahren
presume, to	vermuten
presumption of title	Eigentumsvermutung

prevent, to	verhindern
previously ascertained by law	im Vorhinein gesetzlich bestimmt
prima facie evidence	Beweis des ersten Anscheins
primary source of law	primäre Rechtsquelle
principal	Geschäftsherr
principle of separation and abstraction	Trennungs- und Abstraktionsprinzip
private international law	Internationales Privatrecht
private law	Privatrecht, Zivilrecht
probate court	Nachlassgericht
probation	Bewährung
produce, to	produzieren, herstellen
producer	Hersteller
product liability	Produkthaftung
professionals	Fachleute
profit	Gewinn
prohibit, to	verbieten
promise	Versprechen
property	Eigentum; Sachenrecht
proprietor	Eigentümer
prosecutor	Staatsanwalt, Staatsanwältin
protect, to	schützen
protection	Schutz
protective measure	Schutzmaßnahme
prove, to	beweisen
provide for, to	bereitstellen, gewährleisten, vorsehen
provide that, to	vorsehen dass, regeln, dass, bestimmen
provide with, to	versorgen mit, bereitstellen
provision	Regelung, Bestimmung
public international law	Völkerrecht
public law	Öffentliches Recht
public prosecutor	Staatsanwalt
punish, to	strafen, bestrafen
punishment	Strafe, Bestrafung
punitive damages	Strafschadensersatz (*oder unübersetzt*)
purchase	Kauf
purchase price	Kaufpreis
purchase, to	kaufen
pursuant to	gemäß
pursue, to	verfolgen
put forth, to	vorbringen
put forward, to	vorlegen
put s.o. through to s.b., to	jmd. durchstellen
questioning	Befragung, Verhör

R

rape	Vergewaltigung
rapist	Vergewaltiger
ratification	Ratifikation
ratify, to	ratifizieren
real estate	Grundstück
real property	unbewegliche Sachen

reasoning	Begründung
receivable	Forderung
recognition	Anerkennung
recognize, to	anerkennen
record	Protokoll
refer to, to	sich beziehen auf
references	Zeugnisse (*im Arbeitsrecht*)
refrain from, to	unterlassen
refuse, to	verweigern
regardless of	ungeachtet
register, to	eintragen
registration	Eintragung
regulate, to	regeln
regulation	Verordnung
reject, to	ablehnen
relation	Beziehung
relative	Verwandte(r)
relief	Rechtsbehelf
relinquish possession, to	Besitz aufgeben
remain in possession, to	in Besitz bleiben
remark	Anmerkung
remedy	Klagebegehren, Rechtsmittel, Rechts-behelf
reminder	Mahnung
removal	Verweisung an eine anderes Gericht
render a decision, to	eine Entscheidung erlassen
rent	Miete
represent before court, to	vor Gericht vertreten
represent, to	vertreten, repräsentieren, stellvertreten
request, to	anfragen, anfordern, verlangen
require, to	benötigen, erfordern, fordern
res judicata	Rechtskraft
reservation of title	Eigentumsvorbehalt
resolution	Beschluss
respecting	in Beziehung auf, im Hinblick auf
respectively	beziehungsweise
restraint of competition	Wettbewerbsbeschränkung
restrictive	restriktiv
result	Ergebnis
resume possession, to	Besitz wieder aufnehmen
resume, CV (Curriculum vitae)	Lebenslauf
retailer	Einzelhändler/in
retain, to	zurückbehalten
retention of title	Eigentumsvorbehalt
retreat, to	sich zurückziehen
reverse (a judgment), to	aufheben (ein Urteil)
review, to	besprechen, immer wieder durchgehen
revocation	Widerruf
revoke, to	widerrufen
right to a jury trial	Recht auf eine Verhandlung vor einer Jury
ring binder	Ordner

rise, to	sich erheben
risk	Gefahr
robbery	Raub
Roman Law	Römisches Recht
root	Wurzel, Ursprung
rule of law	Rechtsstaatsgrundsatz
ruler	Lineal

S

safe, to	speichern
salary	Gehalt
sale	Verkauf
sales contract	Kaufvertrag
scholar	Wissenschaftler/in, Gelehrter
scissors	Schere
search	Durchsuchung
secondary source of law	sekundäre Rechtsquelle
second-degree	mit bedingtem Vorsatz (*im Strafrecht*)
security	Wertpapier
security agreement	Sicherungsvertrag, Sicherungsabrede
security interest	Sicherungsrecht
seizure	Beschlagnahme
select, to	auswählen
self-defense	Notwehr
seller	Verkäufer/in
sentence	Urteil (*im Strafrecht*)
sentenced	verurteilt (*im Strafrecht*)
separate, to	trennen
separation	Trennung
separation of powers	Gewaltenteilung
separation of property	Gütertrennung
serve, to	zustellen
service of documents	Zustellung von Dokumenten
set forth, to	darlegen, vorschreiben
set up, to	aufbauen, aufsetzen, verfassen
settlement	Vergleich
shall	muss
shall not	darf nicht
shareholder	Aktionär/in
sheet of paper	Blatt Papier
shift of burden of proof	Beweislastumkehr
ship, to	versenden, abschicken
shoplifting	Ladendiebstahl
sign, to	unterzeichnen
significant	bedeutend
similarly	ähnlich
slander	Verleumdung
slavery	Sklaverei
solicitor	*englischer Anwalt, der die gerichtliche Verhandlung vorbereitet, den Mandanten vor Gericht aber nicht vertritt*

source of law	Rechtsquelle
spare part	Ersatzteil
specific performance	Erfüllung, Vertragserfüllung
speedy and public trial	zügige und öffentliche Verhandlung
spokesman	Sprecher
spokeswoman	Sprecherin
spouse	Ehegatte
standard terms	Allgemeine Geschäftsbedingungen
stapler	Tacker
statute	Gesetz
statute of limitation(s)	Verjährung
steal, to	stehlen
stipulate, to	vertraglich vereinbaren
stipulation	Vertragsbestimmung
stock	Aktie
stock exchange	Börse
strict liability	Gefährdungshaftung
study law, to	Jura studieren
subject-matter jurisdiction	sachliche Zuständigkeit (eines Gerichts)
submit, to	vorlegen
substantive law	materielles Recht
sufficient	hinreichend, ausreichend
suggest, to	vorschlagen
summer associate	*Jurastudent in den USA, der in den law-school-Ferien in einer Kanzlei arbeitet*
summons	Ladung
supply, to	einbringen, beitragen
suretyship	Bürgschaft
surrender possession, to	Besitz aufgeben
suspect	Tatverdächtige(r)
sustain, to	stattgeben
synonym	Synonym

T

take into consideration, to	in Betracht ziehen
take possession, to	Besitz ergreifen
take someone into custody, to	jemanden in Untersuchungshaft nehmen
take the stand, to	den Zeugenstand betreten
taking of evidence	Beweisaufnahme
tangible property	körperliche Gegenstände
tape	Klebstreifen, Tesafilm
tax law	Steuerrecht
tenant	Mieter/in
term	Begriff
termination	Beendigung
territory	Gebiet
testamentary succession	testamentarische Erbfolge
testate succession	testamentarische Erbfolge
the action is pending	die Klage ist rechtshängig
the best interest and welfare of the child	Kindeswohl
the former	Erster/e/es

the right to bear arms	das Recht, Waffen zu tragen
theft	Diebstahl
therefore	daher
thief	Dieb/in
thing	Sache
thus	daher, deshalb
time limit	Frist
title	Eigentum
to a certain degree	zu einem gewissen Grad
tort action	Klage aus unerlaubter Handlung
tortfeasor	Schädiger/in
torts	Deliktsrecht
torture	Folter
trade	Handel
trainee	Auszubildende(r)
transaction	Geschäft
transfer of title	Eigentumsübertragung
transfer property, to	Eigentum übertragen
transferable	abtretbar, übertragbar
treason	Verrat
treatise	Lehrbuch
trespass	Besitzstörung
trial	Gerichtsverhandlung, Verhandlung
trial court	Instanzgericht

U

ultimately	letztendlich, schließlich
unconstitutional	verfassungswidrig
under arrest	in Haft
underlie, to	zugrunde liegen
unemployed	arbeitslos
unfair competition	Unlauterer Wettbewerb
unjust	ungerecht
unjust enrichment	Ungerechtfertigte Bereicherung
unless	es sei denn
unlike	im Gegensatz zu, im Unterschied zu
upon application	auf Antrag
usury	Wucher
utilities	Nebenkosten (*im Mietrecht*)

V

valid	rechtskräftig, wirksam
value	Wert
venue	örtliche Zuständigkeit (eines Gerichts)
verdict	Juryentscheidung
vest power, to	Befugnisse/Macht übertragen
victim	Opfer
views	Ansichten
violate, to	verletzen
violation of duty of care	Sorgfaltspflichtverletzung

void	nichtig, ungültig, unwirksam
voidable	anfechtbar
vote, to	wählen

W

wages	Lohn
waive, to	verzichten
waiver	Verzicht
warranty	Gewährleistung(srecht)
whereas	wohingegen
whereof	dessen
wholesaler	Großhändler/in
wife	Ehefrau
will	Testament
with reference to	mit Bezug zu
withdraw, to	zurücktreten
withhold, to	zurückbehalten
witness	Zeuge, Zeugin
wrong	Unrecht

II. Deutsch – Englisch

A

aber	however
Abgeordnete(r)	delegate
Abkömmling	descendent
Abkürzung	abbreviation
ablehnen	to reject
ablehnen (prozessual)	to challenge
abschaffen	to abolish
Abschreckung	deterrence
absichern	to ensure
Absicht	intention, intent
absichtlich	intentional
Abtreibung	abortion
abtretbar	assignable, transferable
Abtretung	assignment
abweichen von	to deviate from
abweisen	to dismiss
adoptieren	to adopt
Adoption	adoption
Adoptiveltern	adoptive parents
ähnlich	similar(ly)
Akt der Gesetzgebung	legislative act
Akte	file
Aktennotiz	memo
Aktenzeichen	docket number, file number
Aktie	stock
Aktionär/in	shareholder
aktives Tun	act
Allgemeine Geschäftsbedingungen	standard terms, general terms and conditions
Allgemeiner Teil	general part
am Apparat	speaking
am Apparat bleiben	to hold the line
Analogie	analogy
anbieten	to offer
Anbietende(r)	offeror
ändern (ein Gesetz, einen Vertrag)	to amend
anerkennen	to acknowledge, to recognize
Anerkennung	recognition
anfechtbar	voidable
anfordern	to request
anfragen	to request
Angaben	data
Angebot	offer

angeklagt werden (formell)	to be charged with
Angeklagte(r)	accused, defendant
Angeschuldigte(r)	accused
anhängen	to attach
Anhörung	hearing
anklagen (formell)	to bring charges against
anklagen (materiell)	to accuse
Anklagepunkt	accusation
Anklageschrift	indictment
Anknüpfungspunkt (im IPR)	connecting factor
Anmerkung	remark
Annahme	acceptance
annehmen	to adopt
Annehmende(r)	offeree
Annullierung	annulment
Anschuldigung	accusation
Ansichten	views
ansteigen	to increase
Antrag (formell)	motion
Anwalt	attorney, lawyer (*siehe auch unter* „*Rechtsanwalt*")
anwendbar sein auf	to apply to
Anwendbarkeit	applicability
anwenden	to apply
Anwendung	application
Anzahlung	down payment
Arbeitgeber/in	employer
Arbeitnehmer/in	employee
arbeitslos	unemployed
Arbeitsvertrag	employment contract
Arglist	fraud
arglistig	fraudulent
arglistige Täuschung	fraud
Argument	argument
Attentat	assassination
auf Antrag	upon application
auf etwas beruhen	to be based on
auf frischer Tat ertappt werden	to be caught red-handed
auf Grund von	due to
auf Kredit	on credit
aufbauen	to set up
auferlegen	to impose
aufgrund	due to
aufheben (ein Urteil)	to reverse (a judgment)
aufkommen	to arise
auflösen	to dissolve
Auflösung	dissolution
aufrufen	to call
aufsetzen	to set up
aufteilen	to divide
Aufwendungen	expenses
Ausbleiben	failure

ausdrücken	to express
ausdrücklich	express, expressly
ausführende Gewalt	executive, executive power
auslegen	to construe, to interpret
Auslegung	construction, interpretation
Auslieferung	extradition
ausreichend	sufficient
ausschließliche Zuständigkeit	exclusive jurisdiction
außer	except
außervertraglich	non-contractual
ausstellen (ein Dokument)	to issue a document
ausüben	to exercise
auswählen	to select
Auszubildende(r)	trainee

B

Bankrecht	banking law
basieren auf	to be based on
bedeutend	significant
bedingt	conditional
Bedingung	condition
beeinflussen	to influence
beeinträchtigen	to interfere with
Beendigung	completion, termination
befangen	bias
befinden	to find, to hold
befragen	to consult; to examine
befragt werden	be questioned, to
Befragung	interrogation, questioning
Befugnis	power
Befugnisse übertragen	to vest power
begehen	to commit
begrenzt	definite
Begriff	notion; term
Begründung	reasoning
Begünstigte(r)	beneficiary
behaupten	to allege
Behauptung	allegation
Behörde	authority
bei Erhalt der Ware	on receipt of the goods
beinhalten	to include
beitragen	to supply
Beklagte(r)	defendant
Beleidigung	defamation
benennen	to appoint
benötigen	to require
Beratung	deliberation
berechnen	to charge
bereitstellen	to provide for, to provide with
Berufung	appeal
Beschlagnahme	seizure

Beschluss	resolution
beschränkt	limited
Besitz	possession
Besitz aufgeben	to relinquish possession, to surrender possession
Besitz ergreifen	to take possession
Besitz erlangen	to gain possession
Besitzentziehung	dispossession
Besitzer	possessor
Besitzstörung	trespass
besonderer/e/es	particular
besprechen, immer wieder durchgehen	to review
bestätigen	to confirm
bestehen aus	to consist of
bestimmen	to provide
Bestimmung	provision
Bestrafung	punishment
bestreiten	to deny
betrachten	to consider
betrachtet werden	to be considered
Betrug	fraud
betrügerisch	fraudulent
Bevölkerung	population
bewaffnet	armed
bewahren	to preserve
bewegliche Sachen	movable property, personal property
Beweis	evidence
Beweis des ersten Anscheins	prima facie evidence
Beweisaufnahme	taking of evidence
beweisen	to prove
Beweislage	preponderance of evidence
Beweislast	burden of proof
Beweislastumkehr	shift of burden of proof
Bewerbung	application
Bewerbungsgespräch	interview
bewerten	to evaluate
bewiesene Tatsache	fact
Beziehung	relation
beziehungsweise	respectively
Bezirk	district
Bezirksstaatsanwalt	district attorney (DA)
billigen	to approve
bindend	binding
Blatt Papier	sheet of paper
Bleistift	pencil
Börse	stock exchange
böswillig	malicious
Brandstifter/in	arsonist
Brandstiftung	arson
Bundesrecht	federal law
Bürger/in	citizen
Bürgerkrieg	civil war

Bürgerliches Gesetzbuch	Civil Code
Bürgerrecht	civil right
Bürgschaft	suretyship
Bürobedarf	office supply
Büroklammer	paperclip

D

d.h. (das heißt)	i.e. (id est = that is)
daher	therefore, thus, as a result
darf nicht	may not, shall not
darlegen	to set forth
Darlehen	loan
Darlehensgeber/in	lender
Darlehensnehmer/in	borrower
darstellen	to provide for
darüber hinaus	in addition
das beste Ergebnis erzielen	to achieve the best outcome
das Recht, Waffen zu tragen	the right to bear arms
Daten	data (pl.)
delegieren	to delegate
Delegierte(r)	delegate
Delikt	delict, offense
Deliktsrecht	torts, delict
demzufolge	as a result
den Besitz wiederaufnehmen	to resume possession
den Zeugenstand betreten	to take the stand
deshalb	thus
dessen	whereof
die Klage ist rechtshängig	the action is pending
Dieb/in	thief
Diebstahl	theft
Durchsuchung	search
Durchwahl	extension

E

Eckpfeiler	cornerstone
Ehe	marriage
Ehebruch	adultery
Ehefrau	wife
Ehegatte	spouse
ehelicher Güterstand	matrimonial property
Ehemann	husband
Ehevertrag	prenuptial agreement, marriage contract
Eid	oath
eidesstattliche Versicherung	affidavit
Eigentum	ownership, property, title
Eigentum an einem Grundstück übertragen	to convey
Eigentum übertragen	to transfer property

Eigentümer/in	owner, proprietor
Eigentumsübergang	passing of title
Eigentumsübertragung	transfer of title
Eigentumsvermutung	presumption of title
Eigentumsvorbehalt	reservation of title, retention of title
ein Angebot annehmen	to accept an offer
ein Angebot machen	to make an offer
ein Gesetz erlassen	to enact, to pass a law/an act/a statute
ein Recht genießen	to enjoy a right
ein Recht verwirken	to forfeit a right
ein Verbrechen begehen	to commit a crime
Einbrecher/in	burglar
einbringen	to supply
Einbruchdiebstahl	burglary
eine Einrede erheben gegen	to challenge
eine Entscheidung erlassen	to render a decision
eine Klage abweisen	to dismiss an action
eine Versammlung abhalten	to hold a convention
einen Anspruch haben auf	to be entitled to
einen Vertrag schließen	to conclude a contract, to enter into a contract, to make a contract
einer Ansicht folgen	to follow a view
einführen	to introduce
Einigung	agreement
Einrede	defense (AE), defense (BE)
einschränken	to abridge
Einschränkung	limitation
Einspruch	objection
einstweilige Verfügung	injunction
eintragen	to register
Eintragung	registration
Einwanderer, Einwanderin	immigrant
Einwendung	defense (AE), defence (BE)
Einwilligung	consent
Einzelhändler/in	retailer
einzelner/e/es	individual
elterliche Verantwortung	parental responsibility
endgültig	final
entdecken	to discover
Entführung	abduction
entgangener Gewinn	loss of profit
entschädigen	to compensate
Entschädigung	compensation
Entscheidung	decision
Entscheidungsbefugnis	decision-making power
entschlossen sein	to be determined
Entsprechung	equivalent
entstehen	to arise
Entwurf	draft
erachten	to consider
Erbe, Erbin	heir
Erblasser/in	deceased

Erbrecht	inheritance law, law of succession
erfordern	to require
Erfüllung	specific performance
Ergebnis	outcome, result
erhalten	to obtain
erheben	to raise
erklären	to declare
Erklärung	declaration
erlassen	to render
erlauben	to permit
Erlaubnis	permission
ermächtigen	to authorize
Ermessen	discretion
Ermittlung	investigation
ernennen	to appoint
Eröffnungsplädoyer	opening statement
erreichbar	available
Errichtung	establishment, foundation
Ersatzteil	spare part
erschaffen	to create
ersterer/e/es	the former
erstgenannter/e/es	former
erteilen	to grant
Erwerb	acquisition
erwerben	to acquire, to obtain
es sei denn	unless
etwas angeklagt sein	to be charged with
etwas in Betracht ziehen	to take sth. into consideration
etwas schulden	to owe something
etwas unterliegen	to be subject to something
Europarecht	European Community law (E.C. law)

F

Fachleute	professionals
fahrlässig	negligent
fahrlässige Tötung	involuntary manslaughter
Fahrlässigkeit	negligence
Fall	instance, case
fällig	due
Fallrecht	case law
Falschbehauptung	misrepresentation
Familienrecht	family law
Federführung	auspices
fehlerhaft	defective
fehlerhaftes Produkt	defective product
fertigstellen	to complete
Festplatte	hard drive
ff.	et seq.
Folgeschaden	consequential damage
Folter	torture
fordern	to claim, to require

Forderung	claim, demand; receivable
Forderungskauf	factoring
fraglicher/e/es	in question
freie Ausübung	free exercise
Freiheit	freedom, liberty
Freispruch	acquittal
friedlich	peaceable
Frist	time limit, deadline
Fusion	merger

G

gänzlich	entirely
garantieren	to guarantee
Gebiet	territory, area
Gebühr	fee
Gefahr	risk
Gefährdungshaftung	strict liability
Gefahrübergang	passing of risk
Gefängnis	jail, prison
gegen jemanden Anklage erheben	to bring charges against s. o.
Gegenforderung	counterclaim
gegenseitig	mutual
gegenübergestellt werden	to be confronted with
Gehalt	salary
Geldstrafe	fine
Geldwäsche	money laundering
Gelehrte(r)	scholar
gemäß	according to, pursuant to
Genehmigung	approval
gerecht	just
Gerechtigkeit, Rechtsstaat	justice
geregelt sein durch	to be governed by
Gericht	court
Gericht erster Instanz	court of first instance
Gerichtsbezirk i. w. S	jurisdiction
Gerichtsdiener/in	bailiff
Gerichtsentscheidung	court decision, judicial decision
Gerichtskosten	court fees
Gerichtssaal	court room
Gerichtsstandsvereinbarung	choice of court agreement
Gerichtsverhandlung	trial
Geschäftsfähigkeit	legal capacity
Geschäftsführer	managing director, Chief Executive Officer (CEO)
Geschäftsherr	principal
Geschäftsleitung	management
Geschäftspartner/in	business partner
geschehen	to occur
Geschworenenverhandlung	jury trial
Geschworener	juror
Gesellschaft	company, society

Gesellschaftsrecht	company law
Gesetz	act, law, statute
Gesetzentwurf	bill
Gesetzesänderung	amendment of a statute
Gesetzgeber	legislator
Gesetzgebung	legislature
Gesetzgebungsgewalt	legislative power
Gesetzgebungsorgan	legislative body
gesetzliche Erbfolge	intestate succession
gesetztes Recht	positive law
Geständnis	confession
gestatten	to permit
gestehen	to confess
gewährleisten	to provide for
Gewährleistung(srecht)	warranty
Gewahrsam	custody
Gewaltenteilung	separation of powers
Gewerblicher Rechtsschutz	intellectual property
Gewinn	profit
Gewohnheitsrecht	customary law
gewöhnlicher Aufenthalt	habitual residence
Gläubiger/in	creditor
Grad	degree
grobe Fahrlässigkeit	gross negligence
Großhändler/in	wholesaler
gründen	to establish, to found
Gründerväter	founding fathers
Grundrecht	basic right, fundamental right
Grundsatzentscheidung	landmark decision
Grundstück	piece of land, real estate
Grundstückskaufvertrag	contract for the sale of land
günstig	favourable
Gütergemeinschaft	community of property
Gütertrennung	separation of property
gutgläubiger Erwerb	bona fide purchase

H

Haft	custody
haftbar gemacht werden für	to be held liable for
haftbar sein für	to be liable for
Haftbefehl	arrest warrant
halten für	to deem
Handel	trade, commerce
handeln	to act
Handelsrecht	mercantile law
Händler/in	dealer
heimtückisch	malicious
Hersteller/in	manufacturer, producer
herumgeben	to circulate
Hindernis (rechtliches)	impediment
hinreichend	sufficient

Hinterlegung	deposit
Hochverrat	high treason
hybrides Rechtssystem	hybrid legal system
Hypothek	mortgage

I

im engen Sinn	in the narrow sense
im Ergebnis	as a result
im Folgenden	in the following
im Gegensatz zu	unlike, as opposed to
im Hinblick auf	respecting
im Stich lassen	desertion
im Unterschied zu	unlike
im Vergleich zu	in comparison to
im Verlauf	over the course of
im Vorhinein gesetzlich bestimmt	previously ascertained by law
im weiten Sinn	in the broad sense
in Besitz bleiben	to remain in possession
in Betracht ziehen	to take into consideration
in Beziehung auf	respecting
in dem Bestreben etw. zu tun	in an effort to do sth.
in der Praxis	in practice
in Haft	under arrest
in Kraft treten	to enter into effect, to come into force
in Rechnung stellen	to charge
in Übereinstimmung mit	in compliance with
Individualarbeitsrecht	employment law
Inhalt	content
Insolvenzrecht	bankruptcy law
Instanzgericht	trial court
internationale Konvention	international convention
internationale Zuständigkeit (eines Gerichts)	international jurisdiction
internationaler Vertrag	international treaty
Internationales Privatrecht	conflict of laws, private international law
internationales Übereinkommen	international agreement
invitatio ad offerendum	invitation to make an offer
Irrtum	error, mistake

J

Jahrhundert	century
jedoch	however
jemandem etwas entziehen, vorenthalten	to deprive someone of sth.
jemanden für schuldig befinden	to find someone guilty
jemanden in Untersuchungshaft nehmen	to take someone into custody
jemanden verhaften	to arrest someone
jemanden weiterleiten an	to pass s.o. on to s.b.

jemanden etwas übertragen	to confer s.th. on s.o.
jemanden durchstellen	to put s.o. through to s.b.
jemanden ins Kreuzverhör nehmen	to cross-examine s.o.
Judikative	judiciary
Jura studieren	to study law
Jurist/in	lawyer
juristische Person	legal person
juristische Zeitschrift	law journal, law review
juristischer Aufsatz	law (review) article
Juryentscheidung	verdict

K

kann	may
Kanzlei	law firm
Kanzler/in	chancellor
Kartellrecht	antitrust (law)
Kauf	purchase
kaufen	to buy, to purchase
Käufer/in	buyer
Kaufpreis	purchase price
Kaufvertrag	sales contract
Kausalität	causation
Kaution (*im Mietrecht*)	deposit, bail
Kindeswohl	best interest and welfare of the child
Kindesunterhalt	child support
Klage aus unerlaubter Handlung	tort action
Klage erheben	to bring an action, to file a law suit
Klagebegehren	remedy
Klageerwiderung	answer
Kläger/in	plaintiff
Klageschrift	complaint
Klebstreifen	tape
Kollektives Arbeitsrecht	labo(u)r law
Kommentar	commentary
kompensatorischer Schadensersatz	compensatory damages
Kompetenzbereich	jurisdiction
konkludent	implied
konkurrierende Zuständigkeit	concurrent jurisdiction
Konzept	notion, concept
körperliche Gegenstände	chattel, tangible property
körperliche Schäden	physical harm
Körperverletzung	assault, battery
Kreditsicherungsrecht	law of secured transactions
Kriminologie	criminology
Kugelschreiber	ballpen
Kunde, Kundin	customer
kündigen	to cancel

L

Ladendiebstahl	shoplifting
Ladung	summons
Laien	lay people
Lebenslauf	resume, CV (Curriculum vitae)
Lebensunterhalt	maintenance
Lehrbuch	hornbook, treatise
Leihe	loan
letztendlich	ultimately
letztgenannter/e/es	latter
liefern	to deliver
Lineal	ruler
Locher	hole punch
Lohn	wages

M

Macht	power
Macht übertragen	to vest power
Mahnung	reminder
Mandant/in	client
mangelhaft	defective
Maßnahme	measure
materielles Recht	substantive law
maximieren	to maximize
medizinischer Sachverständiger	medical expert
Meineid	perjury
Menschenrecht	human right
Miete	rent
mieten	to lease
Mieter/in	tenant
Mietvertrag	lease
minderes Vergehen, Ordnungs-widrigkeit	misdemeano(u)r
Minderjährige(r)	minor
Minderjährigkeit	minority
mit bedingtem Vorsatz	second-degree
mit Bezug zu	with reference to
Mitglied	member
Mitgliedstaat	Member State
Mittäter/in	accomplice
Mittel	means
mittels	by means of
Mitverschulden	contributory negligence
Mord	homicide, murder
mündlich	orally
muss	shall

N

Nachlass	estate
Nachlassgericht	probate court
Nachricht	note
natürliche Person	natural person
Nebenkosten (*im Mietrecht*)	utilities
Nichterfüllung	non-performance
nichtig	null and void, void
Nichtjurist/in	non-lawyer
nichtsdestotrotz	nevertheless
Niederlassung	branch, place of business
Notar/in	notary
Nothilfe	defense of another
Notizblock	notepad
Notstand	necessity
Notwehr	self-defense
Nutzen	benefit

O

offenlegen	to disclose
Öffentliches Recht	public law
Opfer	victim
Ordner	ring binder
örtliche Zuständigkeit (eines Gerichts)	venue

P

Patentrecht	patent law
Pendant	equivalent
persönlich	in person
Pfand	pledge
Pflicht	duty, obligation
Pflichtteil	forced heirship
Praktiker/in	practitioner
Praktikum	internship, legal training
Präzedenzfall	precedent
Pressefreiheit	freedom of the press
primäre Rechtsquelle	primary source of law
Privatrecht	private law
probation	Bewährung
product liability	Produkthaftung
produzieren	to produce
Protokoll	record
Provision	commission
Prozess	litigation
prozessieren	to litigate
Prozesskostenhilfe	legal aid

Q

Querschnitt	cross section

R

Radiergummi	eraser
Rahmen	frame work
Rat	advice; counsel; council
Rate	instalment
Ratifikation	ratification
ratifizieren	to ratify
Raub	robbery
Recht	law
Recht auf eine Verhandlung vor einer jury	right to a jury trial
rechtfertigen	to justify
Rechtfertigung	justification
rechtliche Grundlage	legal basis
rechtliches Problem	legal problem
rechtmäßig	lawful, legitimate
rechtmäßig verurteilt (*strafrechtlich*)	duly convicted
Rechtsabteilung	legal department
Rechtsbehelf	remedy, relief
Rechtsbeistand	legal assistance
Rechtsgebiet	area of law
Rechtsgeschichte	legal history
Rechtsgrundlage	legal basis
Rechtshängigkeit	lis pendens
Rechtskraft	res judicata
rechtskräftig	valid
Rechtskreis	legal tradition
Rechtslage	legal situation
Rechtmäßigkeit	lawfulness, legitimacy
Rechtsmittel	remedy
Rechtsphilosophie	legal philosophy
rechtsprechende Gewalt	judiciary
Rechtsprechung	case law, common law
Rechtsquelle	source of law
Rechtsstaatsgrundsatz	rule of law
Rechtsstreit	dispute, litigation
Rechtssystem	legal system
rechtsverbindlich	binding
Rechtsvergleichung	comparative law
Rechtsverhältnis	legal relationship
Rechtswahl	choice of law
rechtswirksam	valid
Rechtswörterbuch	legal dictionary
Redefreiheit	freedom of speech
regeln	to provide, to regulate
Regelung	provision
regieren	to govern

Regierung	government
Religionsfreiheit	freedom of religion
repräsentieren	to represent
restriktiv	restrictive
rezipieren	to adopt
Richter/in	judge
Richter/in an einem obersten Gericht	justice
Richterrecht	judge-made law
Römisches Recht	Roman law
Rückzahlung	back-payment

S

Sache	thing
Sachenrecht	property
sachliche Zuständigkeit (eines Gerichts)	subject-matter jurisdiction
Sachverhalt	facts (of the case)
Sachverständige(r)	expert witness
Sammelklage	class action
Schaden	damage, harm, loss
Schadensersatz	damages
Schädiger/in	tortfeasor
schaffen	to create, to establish
Scheidung	divorce
Scheitern	failure
Schenkung	gift
Schere	scissors
Schiedsgerichtsbarkeit	arbitration
Schiedsverfahren	arbitration proceedings
Schirmherrschaft	auspices
schließlich	ultimately
Schmerzensgeld	damages for pain and suffering
Schnellhefter	folder
Schreibtisch	desk
schriftlich	in writing
Schriftsätze	pleadings
Schrifttum	doctrine
Schuld	debt
Schuldner/in	debtor
Schuldrecht	law of obligations
Schutz	protection
schützen	to protect
Schutzmaßnahme	protective measure
schwerer/e/es	first-degree, aggravated
sekundäre Rechtsquelle	secondary source of law
sich ableiten von	to derive from
sich beziehen auf	to refer to
sich einigen über	to agree on
sich ereignen	to occur
sich erheben	to rise
sich erhöhen	to increase
sich konzentrieren auf	to focus on

sich unterscheiden	to differ
sich zurückziehen	to retreat
Sicherheitsleistung	bail
sichern	to ensure
sicherstellen	to ensure
Sicherungsabrede	security agreement
Sicherungsgut	collateral
Sicherungsrecht	security interest
Sicherungsvertrag	security agreement
sittenwidrig	contrary to public policy
Sitzung	meeting
Sklaverei	slavery
Sorgerecht	custody
Sorgfalt	diligence
Sorgfaltspflicht	duty of care
Sorgfaltspflichtverletzung	violation of duty of care
sowohl ... als auch ...	both ... and ...
speichern	to safe
speziell	particular
Spitzer	pencil sharpener
Sprecher	spokesman
Sprecherin	spokeswoman
Staatsanwalt	prosecutor, public prosecutor
Staatsvertrag	international treaty
stammen von	to derive from
stattdessen	instead
stattgeben	to sustain
stehlen	to steal
stellvertreten	to represent
Stellvertreter/in	agent
Stellvertretung	agency
Steuerrecht	tax law
Stiftung	foundation
stillschweigend	implied
stören	to interfere with
Strafe	punishment
Strafe verhängen	to inflict punishment
Strafgefangener	convict
Strafprozessrecht	criminal procedure
Strafrecht	criminal law
Strafschadensersatz	punitive damages
Strafverfahren	criminal proceeding, criminal prosecution
Strafverfolgung	criminal prosecution
Strafverteidiger/in	defense attorney
streiken	to be on strike
Streitigkeit	controversy, dispute
Streitpartei	party
Streitwert	amount in controversy
Synonym	synonym

T

Tacker	stapler
Tarifvertrag	collective agreement
Täter/in	offender
Tatsache	fact
tatsächlicher Schaden	actual damage
Tatverdächtige(r)	suspect
Täuschung	fraud
Termin	appointment
Tesafilm	tape
Testament	will
testamentarische Erbfolge	testamentary succession, testate succession
Textmarker	highlighter
Tinte	ink
Todesstrafe	death penalty, capital punishment
Todesurteil	death sentence
Totschlag	homicide, manslaughter
trennen	to separate
Trennung	separation
Trennungs- und Abstraktionsprinzip	principle of separation and abstraction
Treu und Glauben	good faith
trotzdem	nevertheless

U

u. a. (und andere)	et al.
über jeden vernünftigen Zweifel hinaus	beyond a reasonable doubt
Überstunden	overtime
übertragen	to delegate to
überwiegend	predominantly
überwiegende Beweise	preponderance of evidence
überzeugen	to convince
überzeugend	persuasive
um zu	in order to
umfassen	to encompass, to incorporate
Umschläge	envelopes
Umstand	circumstance, instance
Umweltrecht	environmental law
unabhängig	independent
Unabhängigkeit	independence
Unabhängigkeitserklärung	Declaration of Independence
unbegrenzt	indefinite
unbewegliche Sachen	immovable property, real property
unfreiwillige Dienste	involuntary servitude
ungeachtet	regardless of
ungerecht	unjust
Ungerechtfertigte Bereicherung	unjust enrichment
Ungerechtigkeit	injustice
ungültig	void
unkörperliche Gegenstände	intangible property

Unlauterer Wettbewerb	unfair competition
unparteiisch	impartial
Unrecht	wrong
unteres Gericht	lower court
Unterhalt	maintenance, financial support
Unterhalt(szahlungen) für den Ehegatten	alimony
Unterhaltsverpflichtung	maintenance obligation
Unterlassen	omission
unterlassen	to refrain from
Unternehmen	company
unterscheiden	to draw a distinction
unterschiedlicher/e/es	distinct
unterteilt sein	to be divided
unterzeichnen	to sign
unüberbrückbar	irreconcilable
unverhältnismäßig hoch	excessive
unvermeidbar	inevitable
unwiderlegbar	irrebuttable
unzulässig	inadmissible
Urheberrecht	copyright law
Urkunde	document, deed
Urkundsperson bei der Übertragung des Eigentums an einem Grundstück	conveyancer
Ursprung	root
Urteil	judgment
Urteil (*im Strafrecht*)	sentence

V

Vaterschaft	paternity
verändern	to alter
verankern	to anchor
verbieten	to prohibit
verbinden	to incorporate
Verbindungen abbrechen zu	to cut ties with
Verbraucher/in	consumer
Verbraucherschutz	consumer protection
Verbrechen	crime
Verein	association
Vereinbarung	agreement
Vereitelung	frustration
verfassen	to set up
Verfassung	Constitution
Verfassungsrecht	constitutional law
verfassungswidrig	unconstitutional
Verfassungszusatz	amendment
verfolgen	to persecute, to pursue, to persecute
Vergehen	offense
Vergewaltiger	rapist
Vergewaltigung	rape
Vergleich	settlement

Verhalten	conduct
verhandeln	to negotiate
Verhandlung	negotiation; trial
verhindern	to prevent
Verhör	interrogation, questioning
Verjährung	statute of limitation(s)
Verkauf	sale
Verkäufer/in	seller
verklagt werden wegen	to be sued for
verlangen	to request, to claim, to demand
verletzen	to breach, to infringe, to violate
Verletzung	harm, injury
Verleumdung	slander
Verlobung	engagement
Vermieter/in	landlord
Vermögen	assets; estate
Vermögensgegenstand	asset
vermuten	to assume, to presume, to deem
vernehmen	to examine
Verordnung	regulation
verpflichtet sein	to be obliged
Verpflichtung	obligation
Verrat	treason
versammeln	to assemble
Versäumnisurteil	default judgment
Verschulden	fault
verschuldensabhängige Haftung	fault-based liability
verschuldensunabhängige Haftung	strict liability
versenden	to ship
Versicherungsrecht	insurance law
versorgen mit	to provide with
Versprechen	promise
Versteigerung	auction
Versuch	attempt
vertagen	postpone
Verteidigung	defense (AE), defence (BE)
Vertrag	contract
vertraglich	contractual
vertraglich vereinbaren	to stipulate
Vertragsbestimmung	stipulation
Vertragserfüllung	specific performance
Vertragspartei	party
Vertragsrecht	contracts
Vertragsschluss	conclusion of a contract, formation of a contract
Vertragsverletzung	breach of contract
vertreten	to represent
verüben	to commit
verursachen	to cause
verurteilt (*im Strafrecht*)	sentenced
Verwaltungsrecht	administrative law
Verwandte(r)	relative

verweigern	refuse, to deny
Verweisung an eine anderes Gericht	removal
Verwirkung	forfeiture
Verzicht	waiver
verzichten	to waive
Verzug	default, delay
Verteidigung	defence
Volk	people
Völkerrecht	public international law
vollendet	accomplished
völlig	entirely
Volljährigkeit	majority
Vollmacht	authorization, power of attorney
vollstrecken	to enforce
Vollstreckung	enforcement
von Amts wegen	ex officio
vor Gericht erscheinen	to appear before court
vor Gericht vertreten	to represent before court
vorausgesetzt, dass	provided that
vorbehalten sein	to be reserved to
Vorbestrafte(r)	felon
vorbringen	to put forth
vorenthalten	to deny
Vorhersehbarkeit	foreseeability
vorlegen	to present, to put forward, to submit
Vorsatz	intention
vorsätzlich	intentional
vorschlagen	to suggest
vorschreiben	to set forth
vorsehen	to provide for
vortragen	to present
Vorverfahren	preliminary proceedings
vorzugswürdig	preferable

W

Waffen	arms
wählbar	eligible
wählen	to elect, to vote
Waren	goods
was ... betrifft	as to ...
wegen	due to, on account of
Weisung	instruction
Wert	value
Wertpapier	security
wesentlich	essential
Wettbewerb	competition
Wettbewerbsbeschränkung	restraint of competition
Widerklage	counter claim
Widerruf	revocation
widerrufen	to revoke
Wille	intent

willkürlich	arbitrary
Wirtschaftsrecht	business law, commercial law
Wissenschaftler/in	scholar
wohingegen	whereas
Wohnsitz	domicile
Wucher	usury
Wurzel	root

Z

z. B. (zum Beispiel)	e. g. (exempli gratia)
zahlen	to pay
Zahlung	payment
zahlungsunfähig	insolvent
Zedent/in	assignor
Zessionar/in	assignee
Zeuge, Zeugin	witness
Zeugenaussage	deposition
Zeugnisse (*im Arbeitsrecht*)	references
Ziel	objective, goal
Zinsen	interest
Zinssatz	interest rate
Zivilklage	civil action
Zivilprozessordnung	code of civil procedure
Zivilprozessrecht	civil procedure
Zivilrecht	private law
Zivilsache	civil action
zu einem gewissen Grad	to a certain degree
zu Rate ziehen	to consult
zu seinen Gunsten	in his favour
zu seiner Verteidigung	in his defense
zufällig	accidental
zügige und öffentliche Verhandlung	speedy and public trial
zugrunde liegen	to underlie
zulässig	admissible
zum Ausdruck bringen	to express
zur Sache	on the merits
zurückbehalten	to retain, to withhold
zurücktreten	to withdraw
zusammengesetzt sein aus	to be composed of
zusätzlich	in addition
zusprechen	to award, to grant
Zustand	condition
Zuständigkeit	jurisdiction
zustellen	to serve
Zustellung von Dokumenten	service of documents
zustimmen	to approve
Zwang	coercion
Zwangsarbeit	involuntary servitude
zwingend	compulsory, mandatory